China: Christian students face the Revolution

China: Christian students face the Revolution

David H. Adeney

Inter-Varsity Press

© INTER-VARSITY PRESS

Inter-Varsity Fellowship
39 Bedford Square, London WC1B 3EY

First edition May 1973

ISBN 0 85110 370 7

Made and printed in Great Britain by
Hunt Barnard Printing Ltd., Aylesbury, Bucks

Foreword

'If I were not already a Christian, I think I would be a Communist today,' says a university student during an informal gathering of Asian students. Of the students hearing this remark, some were Christians and the rest were followers of other faiths. Yet no-one said a word to challenge him. Many Asian students today are disillusioned with the politico-social structure of their own countries and see Communism as the only answer to the seemingly insurmountable problems of the Asian masses. While that particular student's reasoning may be or needs to be challenged, he nevertheless sees one thing clearly: that the Christian faith and Communism are ideologically incompatible. Thus when one comes to a vital crisis of decision between the two it is inevitably a matter of either-or.

For nearly two and a half decades Communism has controlled the mainland of China and innumerable Christians have been and are still being confronted with such a vital crisis of decision. It is of the utmost importance that Christians today be intelligently informed about the issues involved and I believe that this book is a significant step forward in this regard.

Mr Adeney is well qualified for the task of recording some of the most significant events and situations concerning the

Chinese Christians who were caught up in the current of the Communist revolution. For many years he served with the China Inland Mission and the Inter-Varsity Christian Fellowship and was actively involved in Chinese student work. During those early and tumultuous years of the revolution the author witnessed the kind of inner struggles, trials and agonizing experiences which are vividly depicted throughout the pages of this book. He is well aware of the material progress achieved in China during the past two decades and recognizes the appeal of Communism, but at the same time he has personally experienced what it means to live under a political system with a basic philosophy which is diametrically opposed to the Christian faith. Thus this book will help us to understand what true Christian discipleship meant for Chinese students who have gone through such an experience. By bringing Communism and the Christian faith under comparison and contrast the author has helped to answer such vital questions as: Can one be a Christian and a Communist at the same time? What should be the Christian attitude toward Communism? How can a Christian serve and witness in a Communist society? What can we learn from the church in China?

I heartily recommend this book to all Christians who dare to think through those issues raised by its author.

Choong Chee Pang

Acknowledgments

I would like to acknowledge with gratitude the help of many who have read through the manuscript and made valuable suggestions, including members of my family, students at the Discipleship Training Centre and fellow-workers in the Inter-Varsity Press, Scripture Union and the Way Press. Special thanks are due to Miss Lorena Tan and Mrs Marvin Dunn for editorial help, to Miss Elsie Lim for typing the manuscript, and also to Choong Chee Pang, formerly a staff worker for the Fellowship of Evangelical Students in Singapore, for contributing the Foreword.

To my wife, Ruth,
and fellow-workers in the China Inter-Varsity Fellowship
who shared the joys and tests of faith
in the student work in Nanking and Shanghai.

Contents

Introduction: Beginning with the Long March

The slender pagoda at Anking (later known as Hwaining) in the province of Anhwei is an outstanding landmark for travellers on the river steamer from Shanghai to Wuhan. For those of us who belonged to the 1934 party of China Inland Mission new workers it marked the end of the month-long journey from England. We were to spend the next six months studying the Chinese language in that ancient walled city.

When we arrived in Shanghai, we read in the newspapers about fighting between the Nationalist forces and the Communist armies, but little did we realize the significance of these events. On 16 October, three weeks before we arrived, the famous Long March which brought Mao Tse-tung and 20,000 of his followers to Yenan, their stronghold in north-west China, had started. Fifteen years later we would watch the victorious Communist armies march through the streets of Shanghai. Thus our service in China spanned the critical years in which the Communist movement was taking root.

During our time in Anking there were roving bands of Communist guerillas operating in the neighbourhood. A week or two after our arrival we had to give up walks in the country, and one day we awoke to find a British gunboat anchored outside the city. At the same time we received the news that two young missionaries, John and Betty Stam, had been beheaded together with a Chinese Christian outside a country town not far away. Their baby daughter was saved through the courageous action of a Chinese evangelist.

We were greatly stirred by this event, and it led us to a fuller dedication of our lives to the Lord Jesus and His church in China. In our desire to prepare for the gospel ministry and become well acquainted with the language and customs of the people, we did not consider the British gunboat stationed outside the city to be very significant. The presence of foreign warships on the Yangtze river was a result of the unequal treaties of the nineteenth century which followed the opium wars. Few of us at that time realized the implications of the gunboat policy through which missionaries were protected by the armed power of the nations to which they belonged. Even though we did not ask for protection and longed to be identified with the land of our adoption, we could not avoid the stigma of being associated with imperialist powers.

We certainly could not say that the fact that we benefited from political treaties which were not fair to China should keep us from preaching the gospel. Missionaries often did not approve of the policies of their government, but they had to accept the political conditions of their day. It was Roman imperialism with its law and order and magnificent road system which opened the lands of the Mediterranean world to the early missionaries of the faith in the first century. Paul himself would claim privileges as a Roman citizen. Political conditions have indeed affected the spread not only of Christianity but also of other religions. The disciple of Christ is called to proclaim the gospel 'in season or out of season', whether conditions be favourable or unfavourable.

Most of that international group of new workers knew little about the growth of Communism in China. Our one concern was to preach the gospel, and for the next few years we would work in country areas among people with little political consciousness. Perhaps in our desire to reach individuals for Christ we were not sufficiently sensitive to the needs of China as a nation. Nonetheless, we felt we could take some small part in bringing not only the gospel but also material relief to those who were suffering.

After spending six months in Anking, we worked for six years in rural areas of Honan province, identifying ourselves as closely as possible with the people. We tried to avoid the large mission stations and went to live in small country churches. A month spent living in the country home of a Chinese Christian was a particularly rewarding experience.

News travelled slowly in those days and we knew little about the battles as the army of Mao Tse-tung fought its way over 6,000 miles of difficult terrain to the mountains of Shensi where the foundations of the future Communist state were to be laid.

Living in the province of Honan, we were out of touch with political movements, but we had ample opportunity of sharing in the development of a church which was growing rapidly. At the same time we saw the suffering of the people during times of war and national disaster. In some areas roving brigand bands preyed upon the people and, while visiting a small church in a place which was attacked by brigands, I had my first experience of being in a town under siege. While preaching in the country districts, we often had brigands in our audience. One evening every able-bodied man was called to defend the walls of the town in which we were having meetings as the brigands gathered to attack. It was a terrible night as we saw the burning villages and fires of the brigand army all around us. The approach of government forces caused the attack to be called off. In those days it was not uncommon to see a man with an ear missing, a sign that he had been held to ransom by the brigands.

In the northern part of Honan the great Yellow river – 'China's Sorrow' – often overflowed her banks and changed her course so that hundreds of thousands lost their homes and lands.

Thousands of refugees from the flooded areas travelled down the main road recently built outside the suburb of Fangcheng where we were living. Together with the local Christians we organized relief work. I well remember the amazing faith of a group of Christians who had lost their homes. They stayed with us and went on their way singing as they wearily carried the remnants of their belongings to lands in the south provided for resettlement by the government. There they immediately set up a little church and set apart one of their members to do the work of evangelism.

It was while we were in Honan that we heard the electrifying news of the coup in Sian at the end of 1936 when Generalissimo Chiang Kai-shek was captured by the 'young marshal' Chang Hsueh-liang and later released after promising that he would devote his efforts to fighting the Japanese and call off all attacks on the Communists.

For the first four years in Honan I was still single. The young woman who was to become my wife came from America about the same time and was also a member of the China Inland Mission. We met at a friend's wedding. At the time it was impossible in that culture for couples to go out for walks alone, so our fellow-missionaries arranged for us to meet secretly in an attic to talk. Later, after a summer holiday in the mountains, we became engaged. After our wedding in Hankow in 1938 at a time when Japanese war planes were attacking the neighbouring city of Wuhan, we returned to Honan and during the next few years before we left for furlough in 1941 we shared in the suffering resulting from the war with Japan.

Our city, after frequent bombings, was attacked by the Japanese army. Again we were faced with the problem of whether to take advantage of privileges resulting from our nationality. A number of Christians took refuge in the church, and they felt that we should paint a Red Cross flag on the roof. The Japanese at that time were respecting foreign property. Were we right to accept such protection? It was not only our lives but the lives of our Chinese fellow-workers and friends that were at stake. As long as I stood at the gate when the Japanese soldiers entered the town, I could keep them out of the church, an ordinary Chinese building with two rooms at one end where we lived, and the neighbouring courtyard where many of the Christians had taken refuge. When the invading army left, after a night of terror, they set fire to the surrounding buildings and we had to fight the fires which could have destroyed the whole street.

Whether it was looking after those wounded during the bombings or speaking to a triumphant group of Christians who were building a new church on the ruins of the one destroyed by the Japanese, we were conscious of a very close fellowship with those who had become our brothers and sisters in Christ. They comforted us when our second child died soon after birth and bade farewell to us when in 1941 we left with our little daughter on the long, hazardous journey to the coast through guerilla territory and Japanese lines. We did not know that we would not see them again. The war kept us out of China for over four years, and when I returned in January 1946 it was to take part in the new evangelical movement, the China Inter-Varsity Christian Fellowship, which had been started in the universities at Chungking.

The following pages outline the growth of this movement – the rise of the Christian witness in the Chinese universities and the subsequent struggles of the Christian students. These events form an integral part of the story of the church in China during the last three decades. If we can understand what lies behind their story – the thinking in the minds of the Christian students, the strategy of the Communist leaders – we shall be in a better position to prepare for the crises through which the church in both Asia and the West may be required to pass in the days just ahead.

Before our enforced absence from China during World War 2, we had seen the sorrow and suffering of the country people. We had also witnessed the living faith of many Christians in scores of churches scattered across the great plain of Honan. Our next assignment was to work with students and share with Christians in the universities the trial of faith that came with the setting up of the Communist régime. We could understand the need to change the structures of society and bring justice and righteous government so that the country people might be delivered from oppression of landlords, famine and the sufferings of war and brigandage. But we also knew that the destruction of freedom to worship the living God and the enforced moulding of their minds into a completely materialistic pattern of thinking was far too high a price to pay.

We believe, however, that the seed of the gospel which has been sown is still bearing fruit. Though it has fallen into the ground and died and the church buildings have gone, the life of Christ remains: the light shone in the darkness and the darkness did not overcome it.

I Before the revolution

'Go where the revolution needs you most' were the characters emblazoned on banners. Carrying them aloft were thousands of slogan-shouting students flushed with idealism and hope born of disillusionment, lisping the tenets of the revolutionary ideology as they sang and danced on the campus of Futan University, Shanghai, in the summer of 1949. I had been invited to the campus to visit the China Inter-Varsity Christian Fellowship group which was large and very active. A few weeks earlier we had witnessed the takeover of the city by the Communist armies. Since then there had been a growing certainty among Christian students that a new era had dawned, bringing with it perhaps trials and testing. But during the 'honeymoon' of Communist rule their apprehensions of living under a Communist régime were allayed by the initial emphasis on democracy and freedom; they had reason to hope that they too might be able to adjust to the new conditions.

The allegiance of the masses had to be won and leaders had to be trained to organize local government and serve in the propaganda corps of the Liberation Army. But there was only a very small nucleus of trained Communists. In order to gain the support of all sections of the population, existing institutions were allowed to continue provided they were purged of all vestiges of imperialism. Freedom of religion was guaranteed. Communist activists, especially in the large cities, moved very cautiously in implementing the teaching of the revolution.

Yet in a way the ground was already prepared for the new seed. Even among Christian students there was a sense of relief that life seemed to be returning to normal after the chaos and tension before the arrival of the well-behaved Communist troops. The students studying at the colleges of Shanghai when the Communists occupied the city had lived through eleven years of war, first the Japanese invasion and then the Civil War. During World War 2 they had been living in a divided nation, separated from their families. Their education had suffered from the hazards of war, as they had been frequently under attack by the Japanese air force. Prolongation of World War 2 into the Civil War brought disillusionment, frustration and often cynicism into the lives of educated youths. For most, the classical religions held no appeal, and many homes were completely agnostic, though the older members of the family often adhered to the forms of traditional religion. But in the lives of the young people there was a vacuum, an emptiness waiting to be filled by some new philosophy of life. The teaching of Marx, Lenin and Mao was to be that philosophy.

The storm raged for many months before the change of government finally came in 1949. Communist leaders recognized that the country could not be won by force of arms alone. In order to organize the masses of the people and promote the revolution, vast numbers of trained young intellectuals would be required. This would be possible only if university centres could be imbued with enthusiasm for the new government. Thus the universities became the focal point of Communist propaganda, and Christian students immediately became involved in dialogue. Communist cell groups were set up in every college and their members battled with pro-government students, while seeking to infiltrate every campus organization including the Christian Fellowships. Picked students were trained by the Communists and sent to every university to wage a ceaseless war against the Nationalist agents who, working through the Youth Corps, sought to bolster up the dwindling power of the old régime. A fair number of the students had no wish to be involved in this conflict, but pressure from both sides made it practically impossible to avoid being drawn into the maelstrom of rival ideologies.

The leaders of the new 'democracy' sought to make use of existing discontent to further their own ends. If there was corruption in the administration of the college, Communist students would lead a movement of protest. When students were unfairly treated or some faculty member inefficient, the Communists organized a strike, convinced of their call to be champions of truth and righteousness. They were especially opposed to the prolongation of the war and kept the students well supplied with stories of the sufferings of the country people and the atrocities committed by government troops. It was not difficult to find examples of bribery and corruption in official circles, and whenever possible great demonstrations of protest were staged. Hundreds of students marched through the streets of the main cities carrying banners, shouting slogans, accompanied by scores of 'bill stickers' who would plaster the walls with propaganda leaflets. Thus they stirred up the populace to oppose the Civil War.

Sometimes these demonstrations would be accompanied by clashes with the police. On one occasion the main street of Nanking was packed with a surging mass of students battling with the police who sought to break up the crowds with their fire-hoses. Such mêlées sometimes resulted in injuries to students. But because casualties on the students' side invariably touched off fresh demonstrations throughout the country, the police were ordered to avoid armed intervention. Even so, accidents did happen and student deputations toured the universities with gruesome stories of police brutality.

Communist leaders endeavoured to infiltrate both the YMCA and the Inter-Varsity Christian Fellowship (IVCF). The YMCA, with its emphasis on social reforms, provided a fruitful field for this type of activity. Constant discussion of social problems gave excellent opportunities for students favouring Communism to spread their propaganda, and not infrequently YMCA leaders were active in the anti-government agitation.

The China Inter-Varsity Christian Fellowship

The China IVCF, although a young movement, was growing rapidly and exerting an increasing influence in the universities. A brief review of its development to this point will set the stage.

My contact with students began when my wife and I were in the province of Honan in 1937 at the beginning of the war. There we met many students on their 'long march' from the cities of the east to the relative safety of the mountains of Szechwan. After our city in Honan was captured by the Japanese army in 1941, we had to leave China.

Four and a half years later I was able to return. In January 1946 I flew over the 'hump' from India to Chungking to take part in a remarkable spiritual movement among the thousands of university students who were crowded into makeshift quarters in that war-time capital. Scores of students attended a conference, and together we slept on the floor of the gymnasium in a university just outside the city. Under the leadership of Calvin Chao, a gifted Chinese evangelist, the China IVCF had come into being the previous summer, and the spirit of revival had spread from college to college. This first winter vacation conference was marked by tremendous fervour as new Christians were welcomed into the kingdom of God. In between the main meetings small groups gathered to pray for non-Christian friends, and day by day the Christian Fellowships in the universities of west China increased in numbers. In the following months we took part in missions and conferences in Kunming, Kweiyang and Chengtu.

I will always remember visiting one large war-time university which was temporarily housed in the country. Revival had broken out among the Christians. We heard about it before we arrived. Even the boatmen of the little ferry-boat over the river in front of the town knew that something had happened because students came and gave them money to make up for the times when they had used forged tickets. The teaching staff knew that lives had been changed because students had confessed cheating in examinations, and one student had even acknowledged that he was using a fake name, for he had entered the university by taking the high school certificate which belonged to a friend.

A year or two later, after the students had returned to the east, I visited another university where some Christians were seeking to start a new group. To my surprise, when I was introduced to the principal he mentioned that he remembered me, for during my visit he had been teaching in the university which had experienced the revival. He was not a Christian and he remarked that he was not even interested in nominal Christianity. But, he said, if the students who wanted to start a Christian Fellowship were like the ones he had met in west China, he would give them his full support.

This work of the Spirit of God at the end of World War 2 made possible the spread of an evangelical witness throughout the universities of China. Students from the first conference in Chungking were soon organizing Christian groups in the universities of the east. In Peking, in the church pastored by Wang Ming-tao, whose story is told later, I met with students returned from Szechwan who arranged the first prayer conference. This was followed by an evangelistic campaign in which many came to know Christ. Thus a witness in the universities of Peking was established.

A month or two later I walked into the Central University in Nanking and asked where I could find the Christian Fellowship.

I was told that they were meeting on the roof of the auditorium. Sure enough, I found a prayer meeting in progress, and as I and two other Chinese staff workers had now moved to Nanking, we had frequent opportunities for fellowship with the group. The China IVCF office was now in Nanking, and my family arrived at the end of the year. I had left them waiting in America until transportation was available.

During 1947 I travelled widely, visiting many of the newly formed groups. One evening I arrived late at night at a government medical college outside a city by the side of the great Yangtze river. The students were not expecting me, but as soon as the Christians knew I had arrived they took me to stay with them in their dormitory. They had returned from the west following the Japanese occupation to find that their buildings were all broken down and furniture was practically nonexistent. We stood around the tables for our meals.

Early in the morning, almost before it was light, the Christians called me to a prayer meeting in a broken-down Japanese fort. It was cold and damp, but there was fervour in the prayers of those young Christians. A year later the numbers had greatly increased, and the morning prayer meeting was held on the flat roof of one of the buildings. In 1949, just before the Communists took control of their city, the Christian students built a small chapel so that they might have a place to meet even if refused permission to use college premises.

In the summer of 1947 students from Christian Fellowships all over China gathered for a great conference in a school situated on the slopes of the beautiful Purple Mountain just outside Nanking. Students from the Central University and other colleges in the area were responsible for making all the arrangements. A day or so before the visitors arrived I went out to the school and found that the students had divided into two groups. One group was busily engaged in sweeping floors, setting up beds and getting the place ready; the other group was praying fervently for the coming conference. Later the two groups changed places. We must have both material and spiritual preparation, they said.

While the witness of the China IVCF in the universities was being built up, in almost all the main universities and colleges the economic and political situation was deteriorating. Runaway inflation and subsequent devaluation of the currency were causing great suffering.

Caught in the middle

During the period immediately preceding the Communist takeover, the IVCF was denounced by the more progressive students who charged them with being reactionary, a hindrance to the progress of the revolution. The Fellowship was the object of suspicion by both the Kuomintang (Nationalists) and the Communist underground workers. Both sought to use it to further their own ends. Christian students were thus forced to face the problem of whether they should become involved as a corporate group in political movements. On the one hand, they realized that if their Christian Fellowship meetings became a forum for political discussions, it could hinder them from bearing a clear testimony to the gospel of the Lord Jesus Christ. Active participation in politics, they felt, could involve them in methods of protest contrary to Christian principles. It could also be exceedingly time-consuming and take all the energy previously devoted to evangelism. On the other hand, they could not be indifferent to the great needs in society nor to the great issues of their day, because they too suffered from the terrible inflation and the uncertainty regarding the future. At any rate, failure to show concern, and unwillingness to stand up and be counted and even to suffer if necessary, would be unworthy of their Christian calling. Christian students, they realized, are bound to proclaim the Word of the Lord against injustice and oppression, for the servants of God in every generation are called to 'love righteousness and hate iniquity'. At the same time they must stand steadfast for the truth of the gospel and be absolutely uncompromising in their refusal to participate in any action which would betray their Christian faith. But while group activities were limited to the witness on campus, individual members were actively involved in the relief of suffering, helping refugees who had fled from the fighting areas.

The IVCF continued to emphasize the need for a radical change of heart which is only possible when the Spirit of God is allowed to enter a human life. The insistence upon the spiritual ministry of the IVCF made infiltration by political agents extremely difficult. They did attend the meetings, but for one whose motives were governed by political considerations to gain a position of leadership was far from easy. The spiritual fervour which characterized the movement could not easily be simulated. A Communist agitator might become prominent in a social discussion group, but in meetings for prayer, testimony and Bible study he was likely to feel like a fish out of water.

One group which had a rather large membership including a number of nominal Christians arranged a three-hour prayer meeting before the election of their officers, feeling that only the true Christians would remain right through the meeting! The importance of maintaining strong evangelical leadership was clearly demonstrated after the 'liberation' when some Christian groups found that Communists had penetrated their committees and were in a position to cause a great deal of trouble.

Behind the IVCF stand was the realization that its main witness must be through the message it proclaimed and through the reality of the fellowship that existed among its members. They knew too that as Christians their decisions were to be made in the light of the principles of God's Word, under guidance of the Holy Spirit, not in the wake of mass hysteria. As Christians they were called to realize that being 'in the world' though 'not of the world' meant that they must identify with those who seek righteousness and oppose evil. They could not be satisfied with a purely passive acceptance, even less an uncritical obedience to those who represented the status quo. Obviously

24

society was ridden with disease. And one response was just as obvious: Christians could take part in a 'healing' ministry in the lives of needy individuals around them. This they did.

But what more could they do? They were a small minority caught between two conflicting political forces, neither of which they could fully support. Any criticism of the government in power would immediately place them under suspicion of being Communist sympathizers and stop their freedom to maintain an evangelistic witness within the university. Some indeed were wrongly accused and arrested. On the other hand, it was equally impossible to join the Communists, who insisted that alleviation of suffering demanded nothing short of changing the very structures of society. The Christians might indeed agree with the need for radical changes, but they were also well aware of the fate of the church in areas that had undergone a Communist revolution. They knew that Communist ideology rejected all religious faith and that a Communist victory would eventually bring persecution to the church.

This did not mean that they would not support reform. But how could reform be brought about? It was quite impossible to accept the fine objectives in the Communist programme while rejecting the methods used to obtain power, methods which frequently could only be regarded as evil by Christians. Communism is a total way of life and demands complete acceptance.

The situation confronting the IVCF was further complicated by the fact that they faced antagonism, not only from both sides of the political spectrum but also from the YMCA. Some of the YMCA leaders were especially bitter in their criticism, accusing the IVCF of reactionary tendencies. At the gate of one university appeared a large poster depicting a cart full of Christians praying and singing while the decrepit old nag that pulled the cart slowly collapsed and died. To them Christians were pre-occupied with prayer meetings and heedless of the fact that society was disintegrating before their eyes.

Then, too, there were a number of 'Christians' who had

turned away from the basic truths of the gospel, joined the Communists and were bitterly attacking the evangelicals. To them it was the social gospel that mattered, and they were prepared to dispense with the supernatural and any claim of Christ which would conflict with Communist teaching.

Students in the Christian Fellowship felt that their main responsibility in the university was to present Christ by their lives and by the spoken witness. Like the early apostles living in a society which was also disintegrating, undermined by countless intrigues and political struggles, they refused to be identified with political parties. Their message was bound to bring change in the lives of those who accepted the Lordship of Christ, but, following in the steps of their Master, they chose the way of suffering and death rather than seeking to change society by the sword.

During the months before the change of government in 1949, Christian students were very much aware that the opportunity to proclaim Christ freely might soon pass away. Their priority would have to be the preaching of the gospel and the building up of a fellowship that would manifest the real love that exists between Christians. At the same time they sought to show their concern for the large mass of the students who were confused and had no clear purpose in life. This concentration on sharing the goods news of life in Christ through personal evangelism, public meetings and conferences resulted in many coming to know Christ, while Christians were strengthened and prepared to witness for their Lord in the days of trial that might lie ahead.

Pressure from the Nationalists

Naturally these large gatherings of Christian students also drew criticism from the Nationalists. During the latter part of Nationalist rule all student activities were looked upon with suspicion. It was incomprehensible that so many students should gather together at conferences simply to study the Bible and partake of fellowship in prayer. Thus while the liberals were openly accusing the IVCF of being a tool of the government reactionary movement, the Nationalists feared that it was providing cover for Communist workers.

During the weeks that preceded the Communist victory in Shanghai, the tension throughout the whole city became almost unbearable. All of the university activities were at a standstill. Large campuses on the outskirts of the city had been taken over by the Nationalist military, and students were scattered, living under very crowded conditions in various parts of the town. Hundreds of them were arrested under suspicion of being in league with the Communists. Many were executed. Undoubtedly large numbers were in sympathy with the Communist 'Liberation Army'. Insufficient food and terrible inflation causing great hardships made the people grasp at any change which they felt might bring an improvement in living conditions.

Shortly before the Communist armies attacked Shanghai, students in one of the universities on the outskirts of the city were moved off campus. One group of Christians carrying all their belongings with them were stopped by the military and immediately came under suspicion because they were carrying a mimeograph machine which they used for their Christian Fellowship letters and notices. One of them had a copy of an old newspaper which had been banned. This was sufficient to cause their arrest.

Some days later the arrested Christian students managed to communicate with one of the IVCF staff members who at that time was living near me at the China Inland Mission headquarters. As a result the Chinese secret police raided our house in the middle of the night. I was with my fellow-worker as they searched his room. Together in the presence of the police officers we knelt by the bed and committed the whole matter to the Lord in prayer. The officer in charge was friendly and gave me the name of the police station to which my friend was being taken. From the beginning he was given special privileges and was spared the ill-treatment and torture that was sometimes meted out.

Before his arrest he had been impressed by a sentence in the message to the church in Smyrna which had come in his regular Bible reading: 'Do not fear what you are about to suffer. Behold, the devil is about to throw some of you into prison, that you may be tested, and for ten days you will have tribulation' (Rev. 2:10). It actually took ten days to get him out of prison. Many were praying for him. It was a great joy later to hear of the opportunities given to him to witness to those who shared the large cell in which he was imprisoned.

The other Christian students who had been arrested narrowly escaped being executed. They were finally released on the eve of the battle for Shanghai, and found their way during the fighting to one of the two houses which the IVCF students were using as centres for their activities.

2 Religious freedom

The battle for Shanghai lasted only a few days. There was a good deal of fighting in the neighbourhood of the IVCF house in Kiangwan, where some of the staff and students who had been released from prison were living. Yet, even in the midst of the battle, we were able to keep in touch by telephone. As soon as the fighting subsided, in fact while a few casualties in the streets were still waiting to be picked up, I made my way on a motor bike to the house. There I shared with the students in praise to God for their deliverance.

Small pockets of resistance still remained, but life soon returned to normal with wild scenes of rejoicing everywhere. Student propaganda groups held open-air meetings throughout the city and plastered the walls with proclamations of the new government. The young especially were swept up by the torrent of propaganda. Anything seemed better than the tension of the past months, and the exemplary behaviour of the incoming troops created an excellent impression.

Pressure from the Communists

On every university campus the underground Communist organization surfaced and prepared for the great task of providing thousands of students to take over government offices and administrative posts under the new authorities. Everywhere catchy Communist songs and dancing accompanied by the rhythmic beating of drums were the order of the day. Under these conditions it was easy to enlist great crowds of students into the political propaganda corps that followed the victorious armies pushing to the south and west. Christians for the most part, however, were hesitant to join these teams, realizing that they might well be required to support propaganda diametrically opposed to what they really believed. Also it was soon clear that, while religious freedom might be granted to the ordinary people, there was no such freedom for those who were in any way associated with the army. Soldiers were usually forbidden to have any contact with the churches, for those who were to take an active part in the revolution must be progressive thinkers unhampered by outdated superstitions. In the cities, however, religious freedom was widely proclaimed. Eighteen months after the arrival of the Communists the general feeling among Christians was one of thankfulness that so large a measure of freedom had been allowed to the church. Especially in large centres, there were more opportunities for preaching the gospel than had been anticipated.

In smaller places the local cadres, with their materialistic and anti-imperialistic training, did not always understand official government policy regarding the granting of religious freedom. Throughout their training they were taught that religion is the opiate of the masses. Furthermore, a good deal of evidence pointed to the close relationship between foreign missionaries and the imperial powers. One missionary, Dr John Leighton Stuart, had become American ambassador. After the collapse of the Nationalist Government, the Voice of America announced the withdrawal of consular offices but said that there were still many American missionaries remaining. A few missionaries unwisely provided information of Communist movements to representatives of their government. Quite a number had close ties with the Nationalist Government.

Even though the majority of missionaries were not involved in any form of political activity, yet in the sight of the Communists they were inevitably regarded as people who opposed the revolution and used religion as a form of cultural aggression. Missionaries whose only desire was to preach the gospel were often shocked to find that they could not separate their Christian vocation from their political background. After leaving China many of us realized that we had not been sufficiently sensitive to the needs of the masses of the people. Nor had we seen clearly enough the danger of the church's being identified with Western Christianity.

It was not surprising, therefore, that the young Communists regarded religion as part of imperialism which must be destroyed at all costs. Chinese Christians suffered because of their close relationship with the missionaries. Only in the larger centres were Communist officials instructed in the importance of avoiding persecution of the Christians which might produce martyrs and strengthen the church's opposition to the government.

'How will the Christian witness in the universities be affected under the new government?' was the question in the minds of Christian students. Would they still be able to continue their Fellowship activities? The government made it clear that the students, like the soldiers, were expected to be progressive thinkers. But in the early days the policy of religious tolerance proved to be of great value to the Christian students, for they were able to claim the right to continue their Christian activities.

In the administration of one university the question arose as to whether Christians should continue to receive the people's grant, a scholarship offered to all students. Usually each application for such a grant was considered by a meeting of the students themselves. In this particular school it was suggested that Christian students should be disqualified from receiving these grants unless they renounced their faith. The Christians replied by packing their bed-rolls and indicating that they would rather leave the university than renounce their faith. The matter came to a head at a mass meeting addressed by representatives from the Board of Education. One of the Communist students said, 'Christians at this university who are receiving state aid say grace at meal-times, giving thanks to God for their food instead of thanking the government. Should they be allowed to continue receiving the people's grant?' The speaker for the Party replied that as religious freedom is guaranteed in the constitution they should be permitted to remain in the university and that probably after further indoctrination they would relinquish their superstitious beliefs.

The policy of religious freedom was obviously open to a variety of interpretations, and it is not surprising that there was considerable confusion. Official statements regarding religious freedom often completely contradicted much of the party propaganda. The paradox caused by conflicting statements may be illustrated by this more recent example. In August 1969 an article in the *Peking Review* quoted Chairman Mao's statement in his work *On Coalition Government*: 'All religions are permitted in China's liberated areas in accordance with the principle of freedom of religious belief. All believers in Protestantism, Catholicism, Islamism, Buddhism and other faiths enjoy the protection of the people's government so long as they are abiding by its laws. Everyone is free to believe or not to believe: neither compulsion nor discrimination is permitted.' The writer of the article went on to say, 'It is our consistent policy to protect the freedom of religious belief and the freedom of not believing in any religion – that is the ABC of all materialism, and consequently of all Marxism.' The writer describes religion as a 'spiritual weapon of the exploiting classes for oppressing, enslaving and exploiting the labouring peoples; it manacles the oppressed classes and prevents them from rebelling against their oppressors. Scientific Communism is the antithesis of religion. Like fire and water the struggle for realization of the ideal of Communism in the whole world is incompatible with the building of the Kingdom of Christ on earth.' In spite of a professed granting of freedom of religion, Communists are told that they must 'criticize and repudiate idealism, monasticism and all kinds of religious obscurantism. ... We are convinced that the time will come when the followers of religious faiths will awake and throw away their idols.'

Religious freedom certainly included the freedom to oppose Christian faith and propagate a militant atheism. But it did not mean that everybody could attend church services. Sundays were often chosen for special political meetings. Only those who were not required to attend these meetings and had no other duty imposed upon them by society were free to be present at church services. Students found it increasingly difficult to attend regular church meetings. It was indeed perfectly clear that freedom of religion did not mean that an individual could govern his whole life and thought by Christian ideas and principles. On the contrary, he had to learn to seek first the ideas and principles of Mao Tse-tung. His Christian faith was going to have to take a second place.

The older people might be allowed the freedom to attend religious services, but the university students were expected to renounce all superstitious beliefs. Intense indoctrination together with a complete organization of their time made it very hard for them to have fellowship with other Christians. This policy of keeping everyone so busy with political meetings that there is little time for personal activities has continued right up to the present time. A Chinese Singaporean who recently visited Peking remarked that people were required to attend political study groups after the day's work was done, and if they should manage later on to meet secretly with other Christians they would be so tired that they would have little strength left for Bible study.

The total claim of Communism on the mind, spirit and time of its followers was obviously incompatible with the loyalty and obedience which the Christian disciple must render to Jesus Christ. Many who insisted on giving priority to their Christian calling were criticized as non-co-operative and non-progressive members of the community. This constant tension constituted one of the severest tests faced by Christian students, even though they were allowed during the early years of the new democracy to claim the religious freedom promised in the constitution.

But not everything in Christianity was considered non-progressive. The Prime Minister Chou En-lai himself acknowledged the value of some Christian teaching and admitted that he had been much impressed by Christ's statement that it is harder for a rich man to enter the kingdom of heaven than for a camel to pass through the eye of a needle. On the other hand, he might also have endorsed the remark of another Communist who criticized Christ's dealing with the rich young ruler. This critic agreed with Christ's demand, but added, 'Jesus allowed the rich young ruler to depart, whereas the Communists would never have allowed him to go. His riches would have been forcibly confiscated.' Thus the Communists frequently distinguished between what they called the 'revolutionary gospel of Jesus' – arbitrarily chosen parts of the gospel which coincided with Communist teaching – and what they called 'a gospel which is an opiate for the individual'. They sought in this way to create within the church a division between the so-called reactionary and progessive forces.

Communism - a religion

To students full of youthful idealism Communism seemed to offer the chance to build a new society. It took the place of all other ideologies and religious beliefs. While claiming to be completely materialistic, Communist leaders recognized that they must produce spiritual qualities in their followers. For this reason we find in Communism a counterfeit for almost every Christian doctrine. The system of materialism has itself become a kind of pseudo-religion. The marks of a religion are usually given as: (1) a doctrine of God, (2) a doctrine of a messiah or chosen revealer of God, (3) a doctrine of man, (4) a doctrine of salvation, and (5) a doctrine of ultimate destiny. Chinese Communism bears all these marks.

God

The true Communist denies the existence of both God and the devil, although he may not always be consistent (as in the Shanghai newspaper which printed a large headline stating that MacArthur was the devil). One Christian student, when asked during a discussion if Communism was the devil, took advantage of this inconsistency and replied, 'If you will kindly define the devil to me then I shall be able to answer your question.'

Denial of God is indeed basic to all Communist belief, and small children in the schools are taught to sing, 'There is no God, there is no devil, so do not be afraid.' The Communist gospel says that God is not love, God is not personal; rather God is inevitable necessity which moves in history to redeem men's bodies and minds from the slavery of hunger and injustice. It is true that Mao Tse-tung himself occasionally uses the word 'God', as when he quotes in the Little Red Book the old Chinese story concerning the old man and the mountain, but he is quick to point out that by 'God' he means the masses of the people. Thus, while Communism has no concept of God as such, it supplies a substitute. Man in society becomes the God of Communism.

The messiah

The Communist equivalent of a saviour or messiah is a composite man, Marx-Lenin-Stalin-Mao, who is regarded as the revealer of the way and the truth of history and who alone has the words of economic life. While no worship of God is permitted in Communism, 800 million Chinese have gone a long way towards the setting up of the cult of Mao-worship. Even in 1950 we listened as students sang extravagant hymns of praise to Chairman Mao. Christian students required to join in the singing of these songs told me that when they came to the words, 'Our eternal liberator, we want no other saviour', many of their number refused to sing.

Many expressions have been used to describe Mao Tse-tung – 'the omnipotent guide', 'the great leader', 'the great teacher', 'the great supreme commander', 'the great helmsman'. The thought of Mao Tse-tung is regarded as 'the sun in our heart, the root of our life, the source of all our strength'. It is said that 'the thoughts of Mao shine on the whole world' and 'to oppose the thought of Mao is to destroy one's life like a moth flying into a flame'. One enthusiast even describes how 'Mao's thought raises the dead'. He is constantly referred to as 'the red sun within our hearts' and is regarded as the giver of new life, the saviour from the oppression of the past and the source of all inspiration for the building of the New China.

Man

The Communist doctrine of man is built upon the shaky foundation of evolutionary theory, and one of the first courses of study compulsory for every student is that which deals with 'the development of society'. The object of this course is to prove that all progress is the result of 'struggle'. (*Lao-tung chuang-tsao shih-chieh*, that is, 'struggle creates the world'.)

Man's descent from the branches of the primeval forest and his gradual development are used to provide evidence for their basic argument that human effort alone is creative. Man by scientific means has created the manifold comforts which have transformed the material world and will bring about a new social order by the united effort of the proletariat. When Christian students in one Chinese university asked a Communist instructor to explain how life developed from inorganic matter, he replied that there was a directive power inherent in man. The Communists were indeed seeking to establish the kingdom of man, and we frequently would hear the slogan, 'Do not worship earth, do not worship heaven, only worship the effort of the people.'

Salvation

Enthusiastic Communist students would sometimes describe their conversion to Communism in terms similar to those used by Christians to describe salvation. A student in Shanghai who claimed to have discovered a worth-while objective in life told a member of the IVCF group that she had received a new joy which she claimed surpassed anything Christians could experience as a result of the filling of the Holy Spirit. Communist salvation involves becoming 'a new man'. It is described as coming out of the darkness of superstition into the light of Chairman Mao. One ardent worshipper in 1969 wrote this hymn of praise: 'Chairman Mao, you are the brilliant sun and we are like sunflowers who are fortunate to bloom under your light. You are a bright star and we are satellites close around you.'

But the Communist concept of salvation differs from the Christian one in that it has no connection with sin in the biblical sense. Communism has no absolute moral standards, for what is wrong today can be right tomorrow and always the end justifies the means. In the Marxist ethic, there is no individual moral responsibility because evil is seen as an accident caused by external factors such as ignorance, social inequalities and man's animal origin. Sin is the result of man's alienation from ultimate reality, which is seen in materialistic terms. Man is alienated from the means of production and from the fruits of production which are rightfully his. Evil can be overthrown only when private ownership is destroyed. From this it is clear that evil springs from the capitalist form of economic relations. When these forms are changed in a classless society, sin is removed. In this utopia lies ultimate salvation. Until the unjust structures are destroyed, man is not responsible for his personal sins. Moreover in attaining the classless society, no action is considered evil if it furthers the revolution.

While Communists do not believe in sin as defined by Christians, they do constantly speak of imperialistic sins. A handbook used in secondary schools in China states that 'the five virtues of the new democracy are love of the fatherland, love of labour, love of the people, love of science and protection of public property'. Failure in any one of these respects is regarded as sin, and forgiveness is based upon confession of these sins. This doctrine has even been embraced by some of the leaders in the Three-Self Movement, whose story is told later. One of them wrote, 'Whoever are with the people, they are God's people, the children of God. Whoever stands in opposition to the people, whether they stand within the church or without, they are the enemies of God. They are the children of the devil.'

Communist salvation is concerned with the transformation of the man and of the society in which he lives. It is to be brought about by social, psychological and educational means. Because of their great emphasis upon scientific technology, the Communists constantly confuse technical possibilities with moral capacity.

Ultimate destiny

The Communists believe that they 'will make all things new'. They look forward to a new earth permeated not by Christian righteousness but by the classless society. This society is to be completely balanced economically and free from all injustice and inequality. Through the thoughts of Mao Tse-tung men are to transform themselves and transform nature to realize the truly human life that in Marxist theory is historically located in the Communist utopia of the future.

Writing in a magazine called *The New Church*, Cheng Chu-hu, son of the president of Hunan Bible Institute, gives this

38

interpretation of 'the new heaven and the new earth': 'Dearly beloved fellow-believers, the New Heaven and the New Earth which we have been constantly yearning for is already here and before our eyes. We ought never again to be confused with the imperialistic visionary view of the end of the world. The so-called New Heaven and New Earth has suddenly – as if by magic – been placed before our eyes. We need but do one thing. We must arise and work. . . . We must positively enter into and take part in the struggle for the People's liberation and demonstrate that they are the masters of the New Heaven and the New Earth . . . determining to purge out the Imperialism in our theology.'

For the Communist there is no future life for the individual and therefore the only form of judgment which he recognizes is that which comes in this life. His reward is the satisfaction that he is having a part in the on-going process which will bring about the future Communist society that later generations will enjoy.

The Communist scriptures
China's millions have become the people of the book. Millions of copies of the Little Red Book and other more extensive selections from the writings of Mao Tse-tung have been used to inspire and control and unite the peoples of China. The Little Red Book was once described as a spiritual atom bomb, and the multitudes testified that they were energized by quotations from Mao's thought. Lin Piao, before his recent disgrace and his death on 13 September 1971, described it as the 'great spiritual strength which will change into a great material force'. Instructions which he gave for its study sound like an introduction to a Bible study manual. He emphasized that it is to be studied 'with a question in mind', that is, the reader is to bring daily problems with him when he reads. There is to be 'living study and living use' so that study and application are combined. Through literacy campaigns and the skilful use of mass media

combined with multitudes of small discussion groups and the enthusiastic testimony of people from all walks of life, it won the hearts and minds of the people. Only very recently it has been discredited, having been described as Lin Piao's distorted and castrated version of Mao thought. The people are now urged to read longer versions of Mao's writings.

Evangelism

Communistic 'evangelistic' methods are strikingly familiar. A group of high-school students voluntarily enrolled in a training course during their vacation, and at the final meeting a call for decision was made. 'How many of you have come from Christian schools ?' was the first question, and a number raised their hands. 'How many have renounced your faith during this course ?' Again some hands were raised in response to this appeal. The final question was then asked, 'How many of you will return to your school and fight actively against Christianity ?' Some of the bitterest opponents of the church have been nominal Christians who have thus renounced their faith.

The Communists fully realize the value of testimony. Not only does it strengthen the convert, but it also has a powerful effect in bolstering the morale of their followers and persuading those who are wavering. Christians in one university told me of the sorrow in their hearts as they listened to a girl, formerly a professing Christian, describe how she had seen the errors of her ways. 'And all the time we listened to her attack we were praying for her', said my friend.

Not only were these testimonies given in meetings, they were also printed in the newspapers. We read letters and testimonies from those who claimed to have been delivered from the burdens of religious superstition.

Mass meetings and other forms of propaganda are not nearly so effective as the personal work done by an enthusiastic believer in scientific materialism. Members of the Christian Fellowship had to be prepared at all times to meet the arguments of their fellow-students. In order to appreciate the difficulties that Christian students face in a Communist society, we must understand the methods used by the Communists. It would be a great mistake to regard Communism merely as a political system. Communism is not only a religion, it is also a dynamic missionary movement aspiring to the conquest of the whole world. Although it professes to be entirely materialistic, scorning idealism and the things of the spirit, it finds itself compelled to cater for the spiritual needs of its followers. It attempts to provide a substitute not only for Christian doctrine and experience but also for many of the methods and activities used in the church. Indeed Communists have often adapted Christian methods and have proved themselves to be more thorough and efficient in using them than the Christians from whom they were borrowed.

3 Tested through indoctrination

Christians who live in a Communist society must undergo a never-ending process of indoctrination. From the window of our room in Shanghai in 1950 we could see small groups of young people studying together early in the morning. The small study group was in fact the very centre of the Communist system, for the Communists never underestimated the value of theory or the importance of thought and discussion. Thought reform is indeed regarded as the means by which the individual is purified and is enabled to experience the Communist version of the new birth.

'Study to show yourself approved unto God', says Paul the apostle, and the Communist replies, 'Study to show yourself approved unto the revolution.' During periods of intense indoctrination, whole days were spent in political discussion. A political lecture might last three hours and be followed by hours of discussion. Students also met in small groups to prepare for their lectures.

In the study groups the first objective was to tear down the wrong ideas and attitudes of the past. According to Karl Marx, all thinking is a reflection of social interest or a reflection of a person's position within society. The Christian students, therefore, had to be 'liberated' from the burdens of their past wrong thinking. Their supposed imperialistic outlook and religious superstitions which had fortified their reactionary attitudes had to be changed. They were regarded as ideologically sick, needing to be healed.

Christians who had not thought through the relationship between their Christian belief and the political and social problems of their day suddenly found that their faith could not be segregated in a compartment of their lives labelled 'religion'. Communism provides a philosophy for the whole man and demands that every area of thought be integrated into one system. Christians who claimed that their lives were built upon the foundation of God's Word and faith in the Lord Jesus had to be prepared to show what should be the Christian view of the political, economic and social issues of their day. There was no room for superficial thinking which divorced theology from everyday life. Their Christian beliefs together with all their past experience and present attitudes had to be honestly exposed to their fellow-students.

Witnessing was no longer an optional activity, nor was it a one-way street in which the Christian proclaimed his faith and looked for acceptance or rejection from his hearer. The Christian student was now the object of 'attack' by those with a materialistic view of life who felt that their responsibility was to liberate the Christian student from the superstition which prevented him from full participation in the revolution. Thus Christians were compelled to enter into dialogue and either to deny or defend their faith. Detailed self-examination was compulsory, for it was supposed to bring about benefits similar to those produced by psychotherapy and spiritual enlightenment.

Self-criticism

The first step in bringing about a change was self-criticism. Not only did the student have to criticize himself, but he also had to be willing for others to criticize him. In fact, he had to

43

expose every area of life to the view of his fellows. His auto-biography revealing every detail of the past had to be written over and over again. Sometimes Christians turned out to be more conscientious than their more progressive friends, like the girl who included references to the fact that her parents had owned a hotel in the mountains. Her friends had told her it would be fatal to include such a confession, but the Communists commended her for her honesty. Students were constantly exhorted to be absolutely 'open' or sincere in everything that they said.

Constant confession did of course lead to dishonesty, as students came to know the kind of things that would be accepted. They were also led to confess certain things simply because they anticipated the accusations that they felt others would likely bring against them. One young Communist who became disillusioned and escaped from China stated that the only way to survive was either by living 'a life of hypocrisy' or by living 'on your knees seeking the slightest excuse for self-criticism'.

Accusations would usually be made in the small groups, but when more serious matters were being dealt with, they might be reserved for public meetings which took place in schools and universities. The purpose of these meetings was to expose those who proved to be reactionary and stubborn. While some Christians gave way under the constant strain of these accusations, others impressed even the Communists by their consistent witness.

A high-school student who came out of China in the 1960s described to me one of these accusation meetings. His name was placarded as one who had committed serious crimes, and he was to be the subject of one of the meetings. It was said that he had had relationships with missionaries in the past and had given out anti-revolutionary leaflets (actually Christian tracts). In addition he had refused to bow to the pictures of the nation's leaders. His trial was postponed until the very end of the week, and much prayer was made for him both by the members of his family and by other Christians in the school.

Two weak Christians were found to make accusations against him. When they had finished speaking, some of the non-Christian students were dissatisfied and accused them of being double-faced. It was obvious that these two accusers were bringing their accusations in order to gain favour for themselves, and the Christian who was being attacked suddenly found that his own case was ignored while his accusers themselves were accused. A violent argument ensued between his accusers and their critics. This discussion took up the whole of the meeting and the week ended without any action being taken against him.

In 1950 some Christian students joined the 'army of liberation political corps'. One girl, during her time of training and for some time afterward, was able to keep in close touch with her Christian friends. Especially at the beginning she had a very hard time because a fellow-student from her college did his utmost to cause trouble, spreading all kinds of false stories and charging that she had entered the corps in order to spread subversive teaching. Finally, however, her consistent life and spirit of service made such an impression that even her tormentor came and apologized.

Her influence upon the group to which she belonged was shown at a large public gathering. A young student who had attended Christian Fellowship meetings – and had even given a testimony at a meeting – renounced his faith and pledged himself to become a progressive follower of the revolution, free from all superstitious beliefs. There was great applause when he sat down. One of the girls in her unit was heard to whisper, 'Don't clap, it will make our "big sister" feel bad.' After the meeting another girl who had failed to witness for Christ came and asked if she could meet with her daily for prayer.

The last news I received from her was contained in a letter written just after a serious truck accident. She had been ill for some time and was being moved to Szechwan. Just before the accident she had climbed down from the truck; the good seat she had occupied in the front was taken by another student and she was forced to take an uncomfortable seat in the rear. A few minutes later the truck crashed and the one who had taken her place was seriously injured. The strain of living constantly in a hostile atmosphere with little if any spiritual fellowship was beginning to tell upon her, and she asked the Christian students to pray that she might be revived and enabled to maintain a true witness.

Thought renewal

In addition to writing out confessions and submitting to intensive questioning from other members of the group, students were required to do intensive study of the works of Chairman Mao. This was part of the drive for a transformed 'new man and new society' to be brought about through the dynamics of 'struggle – criticism – change'. It was constantly emphasized that 'in teaching children, the fundamental thing is to educate them in Mao Tse-tung's thought, so that from an early age they have boundless love for and immense faith in our great leader Chairman Mao'. Generally speaking, Chinese Communists do much more disciplined study of the works of Chairman Mao than Christians do of the teaching of Jesus Christ. One might well question whether, lacking a 'transformed mind' filled with the teaching of Christ, a Christian can ever be a match for the enthusiastic Communist propagandist.

In Communist China it is through consistent study and criticism that students are expected to destroy the influence of the four 'olds' – old ideas, habits, customs and culture. Every student is expected to understand the materialistic philosophy of life. Book knowledge is not sufficient. He must discuss this philosophy fully with other members of his cell and apply its teaching to his own life. He must allow his comrades to examine his thinking to detect any doubts or areas of his mind which may not have been fully submitted to the teaching he has

46

received. Although truth is regarded as relative and not absolute, no deviation from the truth proclaimed by the Communist Party is permissible. The renewing of the mind which the Party demands means that the individual's thought pattern must conform absolutely to the teaching of the Party. One's mind must be closed to all outside influences which might clash with Communist truth.

This involves the overthrow of old traditions and family loyalties. In the past the son obeyed the father and the father the grandfather, but now it is 'no longer a matter of who obeys whom but whose words are not in line with Mao Tse-tung's thought'. If a grandfather's words contradict Mao Tse-tung's thought, it is absolutely justified for his grandson to rebel against him. The Kiangsi Radio in November 1968 reported that a family which had been peaceful before the Cultural Revolution was now divided. The father was revolutionary, the mother conservative and the uncle neutral. Such conflict within the family is regarded as necessary in order to overthrow reactionary elements.

Some Christians were tempted to compromise when they came to the 'thought examination' in which they were required to give an account of their political views and attitudes to Communism. By concealing their religious beliefs, some were able to obtain teaching positions in the schools. On the other hand, one student who insisted in maintaining a clear witness had his graduation certificate stamped 'unfit for employment'.

A fine Christian worker who had attended a compulsory course of indoctrination was asked by a Communist official if there had been any change in his outlook during the course. He had done well in his exams, and the other students spoke highly of his spirit of service; the one black mark against his name was his religious fervour. In replying my friend very plainly stated that, far from being undermined, his faith was firmer than when he had started the course. Utterly disgusted with him, the Communist official turned and said, 'You are too old – this superstition has taken too firm a hold upon you. At any rate do not pass on these religious beliefs to your children. They will be different.' The Communists are prepared to wait until the older generation has died out, for they believe they can win over the youth of the country. This accounts for the tremendous emphasis upon indoctrination in the schools and colleges.

Christian students under pressure

Christian students in the larger cities, where there were fairly large fellowship groups, did not suffer so much persecution as those in the small provincial universities. In one small town the university which had been closed at the time of the change-over of government was reopened under the name 'The University of the Revolution'. When its students returned, they discovered that they had to submit to military discipline and undergo six months of intensive political indoctrination. The whole student body was divided into companies, 120 strong, with ten small groups to each company. The Christians were separated into different groups, and all forms of religious activity were absolutely forbidden. After the first two months they were not even allowed to leave the campus to visit churches in the city. Fellowship between individual Christians became increasingly difficult, and eventually it was almost impossible for them to speak to each other openly. In the group meetings the faith of the Christians was constantly attacked. The weaker ones could not stand the pressure and gradually drifted away. To avoid unnecessary battles with the Communists, Christian friends of one girl suggested that she should avoid discussing the miraculous. However, this conciliatory effort did not pay off because, when she stopped emphasizing the miraculous, the Communists who knew her past arguments then accused her of hiding religious superstition.

About this time the leader of the Christian Fellowship in the university became ill and welcomed the relief it afforded him;

but as soon as he was convalescent the indoctrinators returned to the attack. Because of his Christian witness he was given the nickname 'Pastor' and was frequently told that in this new age no-one should believe such outdated superstitions; they could only lead men along a dark road to disaster. He was informed that all his other problems could be solved if only he would give up his religious beliefs. If he persisted, he would not be allowed to graduate.

For a time he was tempted to despair. He even argued within himself that, because he was saved for eternity, it would not matter if he temporarily gave up his faith. Later on he could go back to the Lord. For two days he compromised, but later at a testimony meeting in Shanghai he told us that he was so miserable that he could not even sleep at night. Finally he went to the group leaders of his company and informed them that though he was willing to serve his country he would rather lose his life than give up his faith. 'The poison has entered too deeply into your system' was the reply, and he was asked if he would be willing to defend himself before the whole 120 in his company. After several months of this constant pressure, he finally escaped and, making his way to a large coastal city, enrolled in another university where there was considerably more freedom.

Medical students in another central China college were passing through similar experiences. All Christian activities in their college were stopped, and the government scholarships which most of them had been receiving were withheld from all who maintained their Christian witness. When this news was received in Shanghai, there was special prayer for them at our IVCF meeting and some of the students sent small gifts as practical evidence of their sympathy. The following is a translation of the letter that was received in reply.

'To the brothers in the Lord in the Shanghai area:
'The letters and money you sent were safely received. I do

not know what words to use to praise His name. Our God is certainly remembering His own children. The grace of God is certainly abundant. Although we do not get the people's grant and others regard it as certain that we will have to discontinue our education and will have to bow our heads in surrender to the world, yet trusting in our loving Lord we have all and abound, and the devil's design has been frustrated. Praise the Lord, God has a very good purpose in calling us to live in this age. He wants us to trust Him alone. Passing through one persecution and testing has only strengthened our faith.'

In such a conflict, however, there are bound to be casualties. The following letter describes how the flourishing Christian group on another campus was forced to stop its activities within the university.

'This past year (1950) the school has forbidden the activities and the existence of any fellowship and we have been told by the responsible comrades that we can attend church only as individuals. We therefore with the help of Pastor Wong have formed a fellowship at a nearby church and continue to meet in his home.

'This past year many brothers of weak faith have given up their profession while other weak brothers, though not giving up their profession, dare not attend meetings. Some brothers have graduated and left us, so that our numbers have decreased. Last winter we were reduced to a feeling of complete helplessness and it seemed our strength was exhausted. We were greatly discouraged.

'But praise God who knew our weakness. He showed us the root cause of our weakness, namely that we were trusting fleshly courage instead of God. Our foundation was sand and we were building with wood, hay and stubble. We were acting in our wisdom. We immediately confessed our sin to

God, beseeching His mercy. Then we quietly reposed ourselves and, like a child with his arms around the father's neck,
rested in the father's arms.

'Praise God, how unsearchable is His wisdom and how
mysterious are His ways! As we began to trust alone, we
passed through our difficulties with ease and a peace which
passes understanding. We shouted hallelujah! The true and
living God who is the same yesterday, today and for ever is
worthy of praise. Thus we gained experience of the fact that
only those who trust Him completely can be victorious. Later
we met many difficulties, but all were overcome as we prayed
earnestly and fasted and called upon the Lord.

'To give all these testimonies would be too much. This is
our experience. We hope you will tell us yours for our mutual
encouragement. I also hope we will pray for each other.'

Where there was a high standard of spiritual life within the
Christian group and the members were bound together in the
fellowship of the gospel, they were able to overcome the
criticism of their opponents. They had to remember, however,
that they were surrounded by ardent Communists who were
on the look-out for 'fringe' Christians – those on the outer edge
of the group who had grown cold spiritually and were dissatisfied and therefore exceedingly vulnerable. If the Fellowship
was alive to its responsibilities, it did its utmost to surround
such students with love and prayer, while at the same time
establishing them in the faith through teaching and through
testimony to the reality and presence of the living Christ.

The Communists had learned this lesson themselves. During
one vacation a girl attended some evangelistic meetings and
was converted. Being a member of the Youth Corps, she realized
that confession of faith in Christ would result in extreme
opposition. The Christians wanted to help her, but she was
closely hedged around by fellow-members of the Youth Corps,
and, fearing persecution, she dared not attend the meetings of

the Christian Fellowship. For weeks the conflict raged in her heart. But finally at the end of the term the crisis came. She was called upon in the 'thought examination' to make a clear statement of what she believed. Either she must clearly acknowledge that she was a Christian or definitely deny her Lord. The prayers of her Christian friends were answered, for she came out boldly on the side of Christ. Immediately the keenest thinker in the party was sent to argue with her, and every effort was made to win her back to the Marxist fold. But she was enabled by the grace of God to stand true to her Lord and openly associate herself with the Christians.

Returning to fellowship

In other instances the closely-knit Communist organization resisted every effort of Christians to win back some former follower who had become bitterly disillusioned and regretted ever having joined the Youth Corps. One Christian medical student told an IVCF staff member that she longed to get back into the Christian Fellowship but members of the Youth Corps to which she now belonged watched her every move and she felt she could not face the persecution that would result if she returned.

Whenever failing Christians are restored, it is usually through the faithful persevering efforts of Christian friends. I well remember writing in 1950 to a leader of a Christian Fellowship. When no reply was forthcoming, inquiry revealed the sad fact that he had drifted away from the Lord. But prayer was constantly made for him by the church, and one day our hearts were gladdened by a telegram that told of his restoration. Later we heard the full story.

Long before he entered the university, he had been in touch with Communism, for his father was a Communist who had been killed by the Nationalists. As a student he heard the gospel and finally became a Christian, taking some responsibility in the local church. Realizing that the change of government would inevitably mean testing, he determined that whatever happened he would remain true to his Lord. Gradually, however, the number of active Christians dwindled, the Fellowship prayer meeting closed down and he himself started to neglect communion with the Lord. This in turn led him to avoid other Christians for fear that they would inquire as to why he no longer attended church services. Gambling and other sins entered into his life, but all the time he was conscious of an inward conflict.

Meanwhile Easter was approaching, and on Good Friday the Spirit of God, moving within him, reminded him of Judas. He felt that he too had betrayed his Lord. On Easter day he decided that he would slip into the church service and listen to the music, though he still believed that the church must eventually be crushed out of existence. But the message of the resurrection of Jesus Christ reminded him that the history of the past 2,000 years testifies to the failure of men and movements that have attempted to destroy the church of the living God.

The next day he met a Christian friend who prayed for him, but he himself still could not pray. Another day passed and his friend came to see him again. This time as they prayed together it seemed to him as if Christ placed His nail-pierced hands on his head. All opposition was broken down, and in the midst of his tears he rededicated himself to God. A little later he had a remarkable dream during which the question was asked, 'Why do you not give the gospel to the multitudes who are dying in their sins?' This led him to spend much time in prayer, and later he was able to take a course in a Bible college which remained open during the first few years of the Communist régime. He is one of many who, in the words of Micah, can say, 'Rejoice not over me, O my enemy; when I fall, I shall rise; when I sit in darkness, the LORD will be a light to me' (Mi. 7:8).

Stories of the testings experienced by the students were often told at the Sunday evening Fellowship meeting attended by seventy or eighty students, all of them crowded into one small room at the IVCF house. Most of the two or three hours were taken up entirely with praise, prayer and testimony, though sometimes a short message was given by a visiting speaker. After a time of singing someone would get up to speak of blessing received during his 'quiet time' from some verse of Scripture. Another would tell of an answer to prayer or speak of the way in which the Lord had given opportunities for campus witness. Another would ask those present to pray about some special difficulty and then everybody would unite in prayer. Often students told of failure, and their stories revealed the way in which the Spirit of Truth was seeking to purify those who serve the holy God.

Sometimes as questions were asked at these meetings, the IVCF staff member or other Christians were able to give an answer or some message that was needed by one who was 'wounded' in the spiritual conflict. Frequently, too, letters were read from those who had gone forth to other parts of China. Thus the members of the Fellowship came to know each other intimately, and anyone who was ill or unable to attend knew that he was missed. If he was in special need, he was sure that other members of the 'family' were praying for him and that someone would visit him.

Testimonies were sometimes given by those who had only very recently come to know Christ. One young man was brought along by a Christian student who had met him while they were travelling together in a bicycle rickshaw. The young man had been converted a few weeks before, when he had seen his rickshaw puller praying on his knees during a time of great danger. A bomb fell close by and others around were wounded, but he and the Christian rickshaw puller were spared. Later, however, the young man drifted away. That afternoon he was on his way elsewhere when he met the Christian student, who persuaded him to come to the meeting. God spoke to him as he listened to the various testimonies, and before the meeting closed he himself was on his feet telling of what God had done for him.

Another student had been so influenced by the propaganda of the Communist Youth Party that he had given up going to the Fellowship meeting. One day he happened to pass the IVCF house as the students were singing some hymns. He had a great longing to go in and see them again but feared that, because he had been out of touch with them for so long, his presence would cause comment. For some time he hesitated, but finally overcoming his reluctance he went in to the back of the meeting room. As he listened to the Christians talking about the Lord they loved, he was brought back to the Saviour.

A book of remembrance was written at those Fellowship meetings so that a record could be kept of answers to prayer and of the way in which lives were transformed through the working of the Holy Spirit: 'Then those who feared the LORD spoke with one another; the LORD heeded and heard them, and a book of remembrance was written before him of those who feared the LORD and thought on his name' (Mal. 3:16).

It was inevitable that these gatherings of Christian students which brought great encouragement to those who were passing through periods of indoctrination would not long be overlooked by the Communists. In some places similar meetings continued for two or three years. But from 1951 on, as Communist control over every aspect of life tightened, students were forbidden to take part in any religious activity outside of churches which were registered by the government. Many valued the fellowship so much that they were prepared to meet in small groups secretly. Large numbers were caught and sent to prison or labour camps, but even up to the present time there is evidence that such groups still exist. Young people coming out of China as late as the summer of 1972 have told of homes in which Christians meet secretly for fellowship.

4 Questions concerning the faith

There was no freedom of silence in Communist China. Christian students were never allowed to keep quiet when matters of religion were being discussed. They were expected to take part in the group discussions, and they were bound to express their opinions of the teaching that was given. If they were known to have a religious background, they were compelled to answer questions designed to ridicule the Christian faith. Of course, many of the questions they were asked were not new, nor are they confined to Communist countries.

Questions and more questions

In the early days of the Communist régime, Christians were constantly taunted with the charge that Christianity is unrealistic: 'You Christians talk about the importance of love, but how can you solve the economic problems of this world through charity? Damn your charity! We want justice.' Christians who had been mainly concerned about preaching the gospel of salvation to the individual found that they now had to explain the relevance of their message to society as a whole. They were expected to have a Christian world-view. Their Communist friends were enthusiastic in their hope of achieving social perfection by destroying private ownership of the means of production and thus producing a classless society. The fulfilment of this vision was of course in the future, not within present history. It is, however, the objective towards which Communists believe all history is moving.

How was the Christian to explain his hope for the future? He was faced with the dilemma of explaining the Christian paradox which his Communist friends found very hard to understand. The Christian idea that man, a free moral agent responsible for his own actions, could believe in a sovereign God who controls all history including man himself was incredible to the Communist. Christianity was accused of being a pacifist movement which does not resist evil. 'How', said a young Communist, 'can Christianity eradicate the system which produces evil when it lacks the quality of struggle which is found in Communism?'

Are Christians passive onlookers while men and women all around them suffer through injustice? The Christian answer is a definite *no*. As 'the light of the world and the salt of the earth', Christians are responsible to call men and women out of the darkness of every form of selfish oppression and corruption into the light of freedom as the sons of God. They are not, however, free to use unrighteous means to attain good ends. Nor can they have any illusions regarding man's own ability to create a just and righteous society. Christian realism and the evidence of history is bound to question the validity of the Communist hope for a future utopia.

It is, however, true that Christians, while accepting social responsibility in theory, have often failed to take practical action. They must admit that frequently they have not shown the love, compassion and courage manifest in the life of the Lord Jesus. Christians will indeed rejoice when they see measures taken to overcome the inequalities in society, but they must question any solution which encourages human pride and independence from God or binds men to the slavery of a materialistic philosophy which denies the right of any other form of thinking.

The Christian does regard life as a battle against all the powers of evil. He must be involved in the struggle, for he expects God to be working now in his own generation. Yet he sees the final victory not as a result of his efforts but of God's intervention through the coming again of Jesus Christ. The call to active participation through serving others, resisting evil and preaching the gospel is accompanied by an identification with his Lord in suffering and a confident hope that there will be a 'new creation' and a 'new man' born, not out of the struggle of the masses, but out of the reconciling work of the Saviour and the power of His resurrection.

Sometimes the discussion would turn to the problem of suffering. 'Why does God allow suffering and evil? If you make a machine and it does not work, you are responsible, not the machine.' To answer such a charge required an understanding of God's gift of free will and man's accountability to his Creator. Christians had to be prepared to explain God's working in history and to describe human destiny in terms of the final victory of Christ.

Some of the Communist students had read the Bible in church schools. They argued that Christianity had hindered social progress and asked, 'Why is slavery not condemned in the Bible?' To them it seemed that Christian moral standards favoured the bourgeois class. 'Is not the church selfish, benefiting only the favoured few and not helping the masses of the people? With its view of an imaginary future kingdom, does it not just provide an opiate for the people, destroying their desire to fight for the revolution?'

Intellectual answers

Christian students spent long hours discussing among themselves how to answer these questions. They could not be ignored. They had to find answers that would satisfy their own consciences and at the same time enable them to reply honestly to their critics. Wu Yung-chuen, the editorial secretary of the China IVCF, felt that something must be done to help the Christian students throughout the country who were struggling with these and many other questions. I well remember the day early in 1950 when he showed me a manuscript that he had prepared and asked me to suggest a title. The Chinese title which we finally chose, *Hsin-yang wên-t'i*, may be translated *Questions Concerning the Faith*.

Mr Wu's book started by discussing the charge that Christians are idealists and are therefore in conflict with Communists, who claim to be materialists. In answer to the question, 'Is the faith of a Christian materialistic or idealistic?' Mr Wu insisted that it is neither. It is realistic.

The Christian does not deny the importance of the material world. Christ's message is for the whole man. In His compassion Jesus ministered to the material needs of men and women, He fed the hungry, He healed the sick. But Jesus also insisted that man 'shall not live by bread alone'. The people of China need food, education, housing, freedom, but even more they need to know God. They have spiritual needs which must be recognized. The record of history shows only too clearly that every effort of man to build utopia apart from God has foundered on the rocks of the basic selfishness of the human heart. The Communist revolution is not sufficiently radical, for it fails to bring a deep and lasting change in the nature of man.

Every discussion concerning the meaning of life eventually comes back to the question of origins, and so Mr Wu sought to answer these questions, 'What is the origin of matter? Which comes first: plan or order, the architect or the builder's blueprint? What is the difference between spirit and matter? Does matter influence spirit or spirit influence matter?' He went on to discuss the difference between the eternal existence of God and the so-called eternal existence of matter. Communism teaches that there is a built-in sense of direction within matter, and it is that which is responsible for the evolutionary development of the human race. But this leads to the question of whether materialism is another form of pantheism. The Communist says that man's effort creates the world. Mr Wu insisted that it is the Word of God which provides the creative power. Other relevant questions, such as 'Is there such a thing as absolute truth ?' were also dealt with in this little book. All the discussion led up to a final chapter on Christ the centre of the Christian faith.

This book was probably the only Christian apologetic published under the Communist régime. Because of the early policy of religious freedom it was possible to distribute the book widely among Christian students. In the summer of 1950 *Questions Concerning the Faith* was lent by a Christian student to one of the Communist group leaders in a large Shanghai university. He was much impressed by its contents and decided to visit some of the Christian Fellowship meetings. One Sunday morning the Fellowship in this university went out for a service and picnic lunch followed by a testimony meeting. He went along with the group, and God spoke to him through the message given. He told some of the Christians that he would like to meet the author of the book. A few days later Mr Wu went with me to an early morning Bible study group, and I was able to introduce him to this young Communist student. A long talk after the meeting finally led to the student's conversion.

Naturally his old friends were very much opposed and finally insisted that he should write a report which would be sent in to the headquarters of the Youth Corps. In his report he said that, though he had enthusiastically welcomed the new régime, he continued to feel that there was something lacking in society. By reading Christian literature, he had become interested in the Christians and when he attended their meetings he discovered a spirit of love which he had not seen anywhere else. He was impressed by the work that they were doing in a nearby camp for refugees from the flooded areas, and he noticed too the way in which the Christian students helped each other. Surely this was what he was looking for. They were indeed members of one family and it was their faith in Christ which made their fellowship so real and practical. He ended by saying that since he had learned of the love of Christ on Calvary he could not give up his new-found faith.

Further evidence of the effectiveness of this little book came in a letter from a medical student in an inland college.

'I want to add a testimony to the book, *Questions Concerning the Faith*. This book has already altered the attitude of a number of people toward Christians. There are many Youth Corps students in our school, and they all are eager to see this book. At first they gave this book to the Youth Corps political teacher specially sent to set our thoughts right. They wanted him to discover parts of the book which were open to criticism, thus giving a handle to argue with the Christians.

'Praise the Lord, "if God be for us, who can be against us?" The outcome was that Mr Huang said, "I cannot give the answer to many of the problems raised in this book. They are certainly worth discussing." The students all think highly of Mr Huang and when they heard him say this they all wanted to borrow the book. As a result, even some of the Christians have still not read it.

'Last term Mr Huang said to the whole school, "Christians are also reasonable young people and we should try our best to get them to join the Youth Corps, leaving them free to preach their religion and pray." He also told the local government that henceforth Christians were not to be persecuted. And so a Christian doctor told us that recently the local government sent a representative to make an apology to him for their previous behaviour to him, saying that their attitude to Christians was wrong.

'Praise God, but for His working, who else could have accomplished so much?'

During the first six-month period editions totalling 60,000 copies were issued, but soon after we left China the book was banned by the government. The author himself was later imprisoned. Earlier he could have escaped from China, but he chose to remain and suffer with the people of God.

Before the government took action to suppress this book, I received the following letter from a Chinese fellow-worker about the end of 1950.

'During the past few months about a thousand letters have been received from parts all over China testifying to the help and blessing they have derived from reading the little book *Questions Concerning the Faith*. So far as I know one professor, Director of the Department of Sociology in —— University has been converted through reading this book.

'An evangelist, Mr——, wrote me that a young atheist, who at first was bitterly opposed to Christianity, had been humbled and brought to the Lord through reading this book. A few days after the young man's conversion, when the evangelist had to leave —— for somewhere else, the young man personally went to the railway station to see him off, with tears of gratitude in his eyes.

'Up to now about 20,000 copies have been printed, sold and distributed, not including the unauthorized editions. Even the Seventh-Day Adventist Church in Shanghai has bought 300 copies and the Catholic Mission has bought 1,500 copies for distribution among their own church members. A Christian organization in ——, without consulting us, printed an unauthorized edition and put it into circulation, and their only plea for excuse was that they could not afford to wait for our permission as they thought the book was so badly needed!

'Dr ——, whom you know well, recently told me that in the summer some non-Christian students in —— University, who were unfavourably disposed toward Christianity, placed the book in the hands of a high-ranking official, asking him to ban it. The official, however, after reading it told the students to leave it alone. As a result, several of the non-Christian students have come over and joined the Christian Fellowship in the school.'

A good deal of emphasis was placed upon the need to understand the arguments of dialectic materialism, for that had to precede any adequate answer from the Christian perspective. There was – and continues to be – no excuse for intellectual laziness, for a Christian is commanded to be ready at any time to give an answer for the hope that is within him. For this reason it is important that Christians honestly face the criticism that comes from the non-Christian world.

Too often we have lived a ghetto-type existence, out of touch with many of the challenging questions which are being discussed in student groups around the world. If reading is limited to a small range of evangelical authors, there is little incentive to face the burning questions of our day or to understand the thinking of a vast number of people whose outlook is diametrically opposed to the Christian view of life. Living in a free society, Christians may choose the intellectual and spiritual climate in which to live, but if political conditions change and they find themselves in a Communist society, they will immediately be confronted by an inescapable challenge to their faith.

Fellowship with the risen Lord
The ability to maintain a true witness does not, however, depend solely upon a grasp of the Christian answer to Communist arguments. More important than wisdom in answering Communist questions is the reality of fellowship with the risen Lord. Intellectual preparation without a burning love for Christ will never provide the courage and steadfast faith which alone can sustain true discipleship. Christians who fail in a

Communist society do so invariably because they have lost touch with the source of their spiritual life.

This fact was expressed in simple terms by a student in Shanghai who had just passed through a five-week indoctrination course, all other lectures having been cancelled. During this special course, which had as one of its objectives 'the changing of the thinking of the Christian students', the members of the Fellowship met each evening to pray and discuss the problems they had faced during the day. They found they could find answers for many of the questions, and they discovered too that they could ask questions which the Communist students were utterly incapable of answering.

This plan proved so satisfactory that one of the non-Christian professors advised the students not to argue with the Christians. 'They are like a glass of cold water,' he said. 'If you leave it alone it remains calm and self-contained, but once you stir it up, it spills and spreads all over the place.' Yet after telling me this, the student went on to say, 'Although we might answer a hundred of their questions, there still would be a hundred and one waiting for a solution.' Being able to answer questions is not really the most important thing. Walking in close fellowship with God is what really counts. A man may argue with a child who is walking with his father in the darkness that, as his father is unseen, he cannot really exist. But the child whose hand is clasped in his father's knows better. He does not need to see his father in order to be certain of his presence.

This was the experience of many of the Christian students during their course of indoctrination. They found that they could not afford to let intellectual doubts fester within their minds. They had to be brought out into the light of fellowship with God and other Christians. They learned an important lesson. If communion with Christ is maintained and there is honest searching for the truth in fellowship with their Christian friends, the temptation to unbelief will be overcome.

Christians were surrounded by Communist students who

urged them to seek the answer for their questions in Mao thought, which the *Liberation Daily* of January 1962 described as 'the moral atom bomb which has unlimited power and can destroy all the old ideas of the exploiting classes'. They were told to study the writings of Chairman Mao with questions in their mind which were to be answered by the application of the principles in the Little Red Book. But the Christians could stand firm in the midst of enthusiasm generated by Communist indoctrination. For a man who knows the power of the Word of God in his own life can say with David, 'Thy word is a lamp to my feet and a light to my path' (Ps. 119: 105). Surrounded by masses chanting slogans from the writing of Mao, facing almost overwhelming questions, the Christian can say with the prophet Habakkuk, 'I will take my stand to watch . . . and look forth to see what he will say to me, and what I will answer' (Hab. 2:1).

5 A church divided

Christian witness in the university must always be closely linked with the work of the local church. Many of the students in Shanghai, Nanking and other large university centres had been converted on campus or in evangelistic missions and conferences. They were then introduced to local churches. During the first two years of the Communist régime (1949-51), student meetings in the universities of Shanghai were able to continue, but later all Christian meetings were ordered to be held in church buildings. It is true that many small cell groups continued outside, but these were frowned upon by the authorities, and later every possible effort was made to destroy this kind of witness.

Christian students naturally were involved in developments within the church. But many of them were very young in the faith, and it was hard for them to understand the confusion in the churches. They saw some Christians yield to outside pressures, denying their faith and joining in the criticism of their former friends. They watched others (especially those with liberal theological views, who felt that Christianity and Communism could be reconciled) agree to purge the church from all imperialism and to change the political thinking of church members in order to bring them into full support of the new society. Evangelical Christians therefore faced not only direct opposition from Communist fellow-students but also serious criticism from leaders of the official church.

The Three-Self Movement

Prior to World War 2 liberal theology had permeated most of the large Christian colleges. The majority of the graduates of these schools soon gave up any profession of Christian faith, but some followed the example of Wu Yao-tsong, a prominent YMCA leader who sought to adapt Christian teaching in order to co-operate with Communism. Even under the Nationalists he had been bitterly opposed to the evangelical message, openly criticizing movements such as the China IVCF and the 'Little Flock', a flourishing indigenous church with which Watchman Nee was connected.

In an article Wu Yao-tsong described his own position as follows:

'During the past thirty years my thinking has experienced two great changes. The first was when I accepted Christianity; from religious doubt I moved to religious faith. The second change was when I accepted the anti-religious principles of social science and combined materialism and religious faith in one philosophy.'

Mr Wu then went on to write about a religious experience in the United States when he became tremendously impressed by the Sermon on the Mount and the fact that Jesus had really practised the teaching which it contained:

'Jesus therefore became so lofty in my eyes that I could not but call him my Saviour. But then problems arose. The Sermon on the Mount is the simplest and most easily understood part or the Bible; it is not a mystical section. Other

67

parts are different; they contain miracles, peculiar figures of speech, supernatural and abstruse ideas. In the Gospels, one event may be reported in contradictory ways. Besides the Bible, there is a Christian theology which directly or indirectly is developed from the Bible, including the doctrines of incarnation, virgin birth, resurrection, Trinity, last judgment, second coming, *etc*. These are irrational and mysterious beliefs which cannot be understood or explained. Pastors admit that they are unintelligible; yet they say: "Only believe, and you will slowly comprehend." No matter how hard I force myself, I cannot accept such beliefs. What originally attracted me and influenced me to accept Christianity was the Sermon on the Mount, Jesus' simple, easily understood, non-mystical teaching. As for these other things, I just do not feel the need of them, and I do not feel that lack of belief in them affects my religious faith.'

Communist leaders gave to Wu Yao-tsong the task of forming a new church which would be entirely free from the influence of imperialism. In 1950 he headed a group of church leaders who met in Peking with the Prime Minister Chou En-lai. I received a full account of this conference because one of the Lutheran pastors who was present asked me to help him translate a Chinese report of the meetings into English. It was significant that Chou En-lai, while promising freedom of religion, reminded the pastors present that if the church later withered away and died of its own accord they should not blame the Communist government.

Following the Peking meeting Wu Yao-tsong, who was appointed the Government Commissar for the church and also a vice-president of the People's Consultative Council, launched a movement commonly known as the Three-Self Movement with a manifesto which, it was claimed, was eventually signed by about 400,000 Protestant Christians. After the outbreak of the Korean War, Wu supervised the formation of the 'Oppose

America Aid Korea Three-Self Reform Movement of the Church of Christ in China' later known as the 'Chinese Christian Three-Self Patriotic Movement'.

On the surface the stated aims of the movement were good. No-one would object to true patriotism, and the Three-Self Principles of the church – self-governing, self-supporting, self-propagating – were most necessary. In fact, they were borrowed from the missionary programme. If these principles had been more fully implemented before the revolution, the church would have been much stronger. Under Communism these principles were of course given a new interpretation, and the whole emphasis was upon destroying imperialistic and anti-socialist influences within the church.

In conferences organized by the Three-Self Movement and in *The Heavenly Wind* (the official church magazine), the teaching of Scripture, evangelism and the building up of the spiritual life of the Christians were almost completely ignored in favour of constant indoctrination regarding the church's attitude to the Communist way of life. Wu Yao-tsong insisted that all aspects of the life of the church, including its hymnology and theology, had been polluted by imperialism. Like all other institutions in a Communist society, the church must become a place of struggle. 'Modernism', he said, 'must oppose fundamentalism.' Progressive elements must purge out reactionary forces in the church, and the poison of imperialistic doctrine must be removed. Following the revolution the only witness among students was carried on by evangelicals who inevitably found themselves accused of being 'non-progressive'.

Christian students, accustomed to the warm fellowship of their IVCF group, discovered that the atmosphere in many of the churches slowly began to change. Instead of being places where the disciples of Jesus Christ were united in one heart and one mind, they became centres of intense political discussion. Instead of working together in fellowship to serve others and to proclaim the message of the risen Christ, they found themselves caught up in accusation meetings in which Christians were expected to attack fellow-Christians. Right political views and loyalty to the Communist Party were of greater importance than the knowledge of Christian truth and love for Jesus Christ. Instead of Bible study there were constant discussions of Communist principles and denunciations of those who were not sufficiently progressive in their thinking.

In the few theological colleges that remained open, political indoctrination took an increasingly important place in the curriculum. Reporting at a Three-Self Conference in 1960 on the theological colleges, Dr Wu Yi-fang stated that the assembled Christians 'had carried through certain adjustments with increasing attention paid to politics'. Not long after this the Peking theological colleges closed, and the few remaining students moved to Nanking.

The path of compromise

From the early days of the revolution Christian students were often disappointed to find that some of their own trusted evangelical leaders were forced to compromise. One prominent evangelical, the Rev. Marcus Cheng, wrote, 'I fully wakened. Only Marx and Lenin and the science of revolution are the tools which will set humanity free. . . . From the heart I can sincerely say that I fervently love Communism and accept the teaching of the Communist Party and the teaching of Mao Tse-tung.'

Later Marcus Cheng, in a speech before the Chinese People's Political Consultative Council which was reported in the *People's Daily* (25 March, 1957), showed that he was becoming disillusioned with the government's policy:

'Some churches have not been allowed to resume services. In small villages and small cities church buildings and furniture have been appropriated by the various government organs and the religious life of Christians interfered with. The policy (of the government) has not been uniform and cadres have taken a hostile attitude throughout, forbidding subscribing money to the church, repairing church buildings or taking in new members. Some cadres have not only not respected religious faith but have even adopted an abusive attitude. . . . The contradiction between belief and unbelief, between atheism and theism is a contradiction among the people and not against an external element.

'We are all citizens of China and this is not a contradiction between friends and enemies of the people. . . . It is a contradiction of the "hundred schools". . . . You speak out your atheism and I will preach my theism and in this controversy you must not take to abusing my mother, defiling my ancestral graves or reviling my ancestors. In the eyes of us Christians God is the supreme being and the churches are His temples, the place where Christians worship Him. In the argument over theism and atheism you must not revile God or blaspheme His name; you must not take churches by force. For example, a letter from a minority tribesman just the other day says: "Our church is still occupied and is in a terrible condition and it is being used as a stable." This defiling of churches is like defiling our ancestral graves and impresses us very painfully. At the opening of a new steel bridge an official of high rank gave an address in which he emphasized that this bridge had been made by human effort and was no work of any so-called God. Then he said, "You Christians should throw your God into the dung heap." Such blasphemy of God is, in the eyes of Christians, worse than reviling one's mother. This is not criticism, but abuse of religion.'

Marcus Cheng spoke as a member of the Consultative Committee and a staunch supporter of the Three-Self Movement. But now he was disillusioned with the developments in the church, and he must have known that his criticism of the government could only result in his own downfall.

Another evangelical pastor who was greatly loved by Christian students and had been a frequent speaker at IVCF conferences went through an agony of inner conflict. He was regarded as a leader of what the Communist directives described as 'the spiritually-minded' party which was known to oppose the Three-Self Movement. In 1950 he was ordered to make a broadcast denouncing missionaries and imperialistic elements in the church.

A good deal of evidence could be produced by the Communists indicating that foreign missionaries had been used by the powers of imperialism. It is true that only a very few had been actively engaged in politics, but it was well known that missionaries had been in favour of Chiang Kai-shek's government and opposed to Communism. If Pastor Yang Shao-tang had refused to make the broadcast, it would have meant imprisonment on a political charge, for he would have been accused of being a traitor and an enemy of the people. He told me of the hours he spent agonizing over the preparation of the script which had to be written many times before it satisfied the authorities. He finally decided that it was better to remain free as a shepherd of the flock of God than to refuse to co-operate and go to prison.

We can indeed sympathize with him in this terribly difficult choice which was only the beginning of a long series of trials. He was a deeply spiritual man with a very sensitive conscience, and large numbers of students had come to know Christ through his ministry. It came therefore as a great shock when members of his own church in Nanking arranged an accusation meeting in which very serious charges were brought against him. Actually Communist agents had infiltrated the church and had collected quotations from a series of messages that he had given on prophecy which could be twisted to indicate that he had preached against Communism. Any preaching of the second coming of Christ or reference to the darkness of society was considered to be reactionary.

At the end of days of struggle in the accusation meetings, Pastor Yang was broken and actually felt that his ministry was finished. He said that if he was guilty of the charges that were brought against him it would be better for him to die. But the Communists had other plans for him. They apologized for the excessive zeal of those who had brought charges against him in the Nanking church and offered to set him free and allow him to continue as pastor of his church in Shanghai if he would join the Three-Self Movement. They realized the extent of his influence among students and felt that an evangelical leader was needed in the Three-Self Movement.

Again he realized that if he refused he would be imprisoned on a political charge. And so, feeling that the church needed his ministry, he acceded to their request. He found himself more and more involved in the implementing of Communist policy, a great amount of time being taken up in indoctrination classes. He was teaching in a Bible school, and sometimes he would come to his students after an almost sleepless night with the confession that political discussions had taken up so much time that he had been quite unable to prepare. Some of the keen young students in his church were bitterly disappointed because of what they regarded as compromise in his ministry.

His sincere desire to preach the gospel faithfully while at the same time seeking to satisfy the demands of the Communists within the Three-Self Movement caused almost unbearable tension. For several years he remained a leader in the church as the Three-Self Movement officials sought to use him to draw in evangelicals. The time came, however, when he was no longer regarded as necessary and he was then accused of being insincere and of 'leaning to one side'. He was deprived of his church and forbidden to preach. But in view of his past services he was spared the rigours of labour camps and allowed to work for the government as a translator until the time of his death in the late sixties. I shall always thank God for all that his Christ-like life and friendship meant to me during my time in China.

The path of independence

His story is in marked contrast to that of his good friend Wang Ming-tao. Whereas Yang Shao-tang had worked closely with missionaries and therefore was vulnerable to Communist attack, Wang Ming-tao had always maintained a strongly independent position. He welcomed missionaries to his church but hardly ever gave up his pulpit to speakers from overseas. Furthermore, he refused to join any organization outside his own church.

Many remembered his courageous witness under the Japanese régime when he had risked his life in order to maintain the purity of the gospel. He would not join the North China Church Union sponsored by the Japanese militarists, nor did he allow a picture of the Japanese Emperor to appear in his church. He was therefore completely consistent when he refused to enter the Three-Self Movement and rejected the demand that a picture of Mao Tse-tung should have an honoured place in his church building. He pointed out that he did not even have a picture of Jesus Christ in his church.

He was not, however, content just to maintain a biblical ministry in his own church. He felt called to strengthen the faith of Christians throughout the country and so continued to publish a magazine and to send booklets to churches all over China. None of his publications would print any form of Communist propaganda, and he strongly denounced church leaders who ceased to preach the whole counsel of God. He criticized those who were unequally yoked with unbelievers and warned that if the basic doctrines of the faith were sacrificed, the church, though outwardly continuing its services, would already be destroyed. If it once accepted the complete control of an atheistic government and compromised in matters of truth and practice, it would cease to be the true church of Jesus Christ. He insisted that the real issue was not political but doctrinal.

In one of his messages to Christians he pointed out that 'in the Scriptures there is nothing but the bare truth of God without any "imperialistic poison" ... We must go on believing and preaching it. Nobody can interfere with us and nobody can forbid us to do it. We are willing to pay any price to preserve the Word of God, and we are equally willing to sacrifice anything in order to preach the Word of God.'

Students continued to flock to his church. His writings were eagerly read by evangelicals all over the country. When no printer dared to publish his magazine, he personally set his own type and printed his own magazines and booklets.

Naturally, the Communists would not tolerate such outspoken criticism of the official church, but because Wang Ming-tao could not easily be labelled as an 'agent of imperialism' and was so well known throughout the country, they did not want to arrest him without public support and denunciation of his crimes by his own people. His condemnation had to come from within the church.

The first attempt was made in the spring of 1954 when the Three-Self Movement ordered every church and Christian organization in Peking to send representatives to attend a meeting at which Mr Wang was to be accused. Many charges were brought against him and he was declared a danger to the the whole Christian cause. His accusers demanded the death penalty or at least imprisonment, but not more than one quarter of those present gave their assent. Following the meeting, the Evangelical Student Fellowship in Peking started the 'Oppose the Persecution of Wang Ming-tao Movement', and this spread to churches and organizations not only in Peking but also in Shanghai and Tientsin. Throughout the country large numbers of young Christians were inspired by his courageous witness.

When the Three-Self Movement met in Peking in May 1955 for the Fourth Annual Conference, some of the leaders determined to make a last effort to win Wang Ming-tao, but he refused to meet with them. This precipitated a violent storm of attack against him in both the religious and secular press all over China. Study groups were set up in the churches to discuss accusations against Wang Ming-tao. Christians were forced to declare whether they were for or against him.

Everything was being prepared for his arrest. Undoubtedly he realized that his time had come when he preached his final sermon on 7 August 1955. At the same time he distributed his last manifesto entitled 'We Because of Our Faith'. In it he distinguished between those who accepted the authority of God's Word and lived in submission to it and those who criticized the Scriptures and compromised regarding the truth. The following extract shows how strongly he felt:

'I cannot look at these men who confuse the true teaching of the Lord and corrupt the church of God without wanting at the same time to throw everything I have into the struggle against them. . . . I would like my readers to understand this: each one of us has freedom of belief. We should respect the beliefs of others, and others should respect our beliefs. But this applies only to religious beliefs different from ours. If someone believes in another religion or in no religion we should not attack him, just as believers in other religions or no religion should not attack us. However, we cannot hold this same attitude towards the 'party of unbelievers' inside the church. These people have no faith . . . Every single Christian is under obligation to rise up and expose the real features of these false Christians and to resist them and make it impossible for them to injure the flock of God.'

A few days later one of the students from his church wrote concerning his arrest: 'Mr Wang was arrested about one o'clock in the morning of 8 August. On 7 August, Wang Ming-tao had given his last message. It was entitled "They in This Manner Betrayed Jesus". The Spirit of God made him understand the things that were coming to pass. His spirit would be faithful to Jesus even unto death.' Eighteen other Christians, including some of the students from his church, were arrested at the same time.

No man had had a greater influence among students than Wang Ming-tao. I was with him for the first Prayer Conference for Evangelical Students which was held in his church in Peking in the summer of 1946, soon after students had made their way from Szechwan back to their old universities at the close of the war. These conferences continued each year till 1955. I will not easily forget the last time of prayer and fellowship with him in August 1950 in Tientsin when we were on the way out of China. He presented us with his autobiography which had just been published on the occasion of his fiftieth birthday.

With his arrest five years later the witness of a valiant servant of the Lord was silenced. With two men always with him in his cell he went through extreme brain-washing techniques which were used to make him sign a confession of his imperialistic sins. After his release, broken in mind, he could only wander about murmuring, 'I am Peter' or 'I am Judas'. But then strength returned, and he went to the authorities and recanted his former confession. Once more he and his wife went to prison. Reliable news which we received in 1971 indicates that in the summer of 1971 he was still in a labour camp in north China. In a letter to relatives written about this time, he eluded the censors' ban on references to religion by adding to news of his physical health the words, 'Do not be anxious about me; I am of more value than many sparrows.'

His example inspired numbers of Christians to remain faithful to the very end. Christian students saw a man who was not afraid to stand out boldly for the truth, even though condemned by many who bore the name of Christ. Mr Wang had seen clearly that even the smallest compromise would open the way for further retreats from the truth. For him loyalty to Jesus Christ had to have precedence over all other loyalty. Obedience to the demands of Jesus Christ inevitably brought him into conflict with the secular state. He knew full well that the course he was taking could only lead to prison, and his bag was always packed, ready for the time when the call should come.

The tightening of Communist control

Mr Wang's arrest in 1955 heralded the start of a great campaign against evangelicals throughout the country. Many were sent to prison and labour camps. The Three-Self Movement magazine, *The Heavenly Wind*, continued to print articles criticizing Wang Ming-tao and those who supported him. Because of the widespread support for Mr Wang, Christian workers throughout the country were required to express their personal condemnation of him and their approval of the action taken. Students who had been inspired by Wang Ming-tao's courageous witness now found themselves under great pressure. If they belonged to a church, they were forced to take part in study groups in which Mr Wang's beliefs were criticized. If they showed sympathy with his message, they were liable to be sent to a labour camp.

After meetings on the university campus had been banned, some of the students borrowed nearby church buildings, but this was only possible when the leadership of the church was sympathetic. Now that most of the evangelical leaders were either in prison or disgraced, Communist control over the church tightened, and evangelical students faced a difficult choice. In spite of the unsatisfying nature of the church services, they could remain within the organized church and submit to the political religious courses of indoctrination or they could withdraw from the church and meet secretly and risk imprisonment if their meetings were betrayed to the government. Some who maintained their attendance at church were also members of secret fellowship groups. Following Wang Ming-tao's arrest a decree was issued making illegal all Christian activities outside the jurisdiction of the Three-Self Movement. Books by Wang Ming-tao were confiscated.

Some real Christians chose to remain in the church and go

through endless courses of indoctrination. They saw their pastors struggling under all kinds of political pressures. Sunday schools were abolished, and some of their friends committed suicide because of the accusation meetings. In Shanghai many of the students belonged to the 'Little Flock', an indigenous movement containing a very great number of Christians scattered throughout China. Terrible charges had been brought against their leader, Watchman Nee (Nee To-sheng), and he was sentenced to a fifteen-year prison term in 1952. He was still in prison in April 1972 and died on 1 June. Refusing to sign a confession, he remained faithful until the end.

There was no truth in stories spread about his mutilation but he suffered much from a chronic illness. In a letter written in April 1972 which I read when his sister came to Singapore in July, he spoke of his physical suffering and then added the words, 'but my heart is full of joy'. The Chinese characters used in this phrase, which he repeated again in wishing the same for his sister, are exactly the same as those used for the words of the Lord Jesus when he said, 'that your joy may be full' (Jn. 15:11).

A few months after Wang Ming-tao's arrest, the leaders of the 'Little Flock' in Shanghai were also arrested, and 25,000 Christians were summoned to a mass denunciation meeting. All the members of the 'Little Flock' had to go through a special indoctrination course and a 'reformed' 'Little Flock' was taken into the Three-Self Movement.

Outward opposition to the government-sponsored church had now been overcome and leadership was completely in the hands of men and women who had been well indoctrinated and had fully accepted the government's religious policy. Those who remained in the official church enjoyed a measure of freedom for a time, while others who met secretly outside were in constant danger of arrest. But peace within the official church was to be short-lived.

In 1967, the Cultural Revolution accompanied by the rampage of the Red Guards completely changed the situation. The church was now regarded as a part of the old tradition and ways of thinking which must be completely crushed. Church buildings were closed and desecrated. Christians were humiliated. Bibles and other Christian books were burned. Christian homes were ransacked by zealous Red Guards eager to seek out and destroy everything connected with religious observances. The Christian population within prisons and labour camps increased. Those who had sought to survive through holding membership in the Three-Self Movement now found themselves obliged either to deny the faith or join with secret disciples in hidden cell groups.

For some real Christians who had bought physical safety at the cost of the loss of peace of mind the moment of truth had come. They realized they had betrayed their Lord and their fellow-Christians. The so-called 'freedom of religion' was only temporary, and they too had to face persecution, if they were to continue in the faith. At least the issue was now clear. Christian faith must be maintained in secret. Only those who were prepared to suffer could remain true to their Lord.

I talked recently with a keen Christian student who escaped from China in 1968, in the middle of the Cultural Revolution. His mother has been in and out of prison because of her untiring efforts to visit and encourage little groups of believers meeting late at night in Christian homes. And still she sends out a call to pray for the church in China. Her son is living evidence of the existence of God's church in China today, for he was born and grew up under Communism.

Undoubtedly the witness of Christian homes in the fifties has contributed to the vitality of the underground church in the seventies. When nominal Christians became hopelessly compromised, it was the young people who maintained the living Christian fellowship. The organization within the universities has been destroyed, but Christian students of those days and their children are a part of the true church whose light continues to shine in the darkness.

6 The future of Christian witness in Communist countries

Can a Christian witness be maintained, not only in China but also in other countries where a Communist government is in control? Obviously Communist attitudes vary from place to place. This is evident in Europe. Even in such a vast country as China it is impossible to generalize. Conditions may change because of local leadership, and political pressures from outside may cause modification of past policies. It may be expedient for the Communist government to have a Christian church open in Peking or Shanghai because visitors from other countries are always told that there is complete religious freedom. But in 1972 a Christian member of a guided tour, after hearing about the government's policy of religious freedom, managed to get away early in the morning before the full programme of the day to look at a church in Shanghai which he had seen from a distance. He found that it was being used as a factory.

Those who go on official tours will find little trace of any Christian witness. They may, like one recent visitor, see 'crossless' church buildings in the cities and be told that a church converted to a hospital is much more useful, but those who tread the way of the cross are out of sight.

The challenge to Chinese Christians

Recently, a young Chinese Christian medical student talked to me about going to live in China. He asked what would be involved if he were to settle down as a Christian witness in the People's Republic. I suggested that he would have to be prepared to suffer.

First, the Christian who prepares to live in China must be under no illusion about the cost of witnessing to the living God. The glowing stories of material progress and independence from outside imperialism cannot cover up the terrible price paid in terms of bondage of spirit, regimented thinking and the persecution of all who do not conform to the Communist philosophy of life. Those who write about China often seem to stress either the great achievement in the social and economic realms or the evils of Communism as a system. Without appreciation of the former, it would be almost impossible for a Chinese Christian to survive in China. But if he does not understand the spiritual conflict that is raging and the evil inherent in any human system (be it capitalist or Communist) that rejects God, he will be in no position to serve as an ambassador for Christ under a hostile régime.

Chinese Christians touring China have remarked on the sense of pride in the fact that any problem can be overcome without any dependence upon outside help. The old religions are therefore no longer needed, and the Communists proudly point out that all signs of religion in the homes of the people have been wiped out. It is interesting to notice, however, that a great many non-Christian Chinese who have escaped to Hong Kong mention when interviewed that they have prayed to God in the midst of danger. Outward signs of religion may disappear, but the deep-seated consciousness of God is not so easily destroyed.

Among the large numbers fleeing from the mainland every month the most common phrase used to describe the reason for their departure is *muh iu chuh lu*—'there is no way out'.

Perhaps this statement refers primarily to the lack of any hope of improving their material situation, for example, an unwillingness to devote their lives to working in the rural areas when they dreamed of an education leading to a more interesting career. The problem of human selfishness is not so easily solved. After all the indoctrination, the shouting of countless slogans and ceaseless study of the works of Chairman Mao, there comes a sense of emptiness and a realization that the road of Communism leads to a meaningless conformity, to a stereotyped pattern of life with no hope beyond that of becoming a 'stainless screw in the locomotive of the revolution'.

The great numbers of those who end their days in prisons and labour camps and the numerous graves of those who have been executed bear testimony to the fact that 'non-conformity' is a luxury which Communist China cannot afford. Even more tragic is the realization that a great nation is building her society on a foundation of hatred of all other systems which do not fully conform to the atheistic philosophy of Communism. Those who dare to disagree with the official teaching of the Chinese Communist Party are immediately labelled as 'enemies of the people', 'reactionary', 'revisionist' or 'counter-revolutionary'. (There are, of course, non-Communist countries too where extreme regimentation of thought penalizes those with non-conformist attitudes.)

Second, a returning Chinese Christian would have to identify completely with his own people. Their thinking would be quite strange to him, for those under thirty know nothing except education under Communism. They are completely unfamiliar with any other thought system, for they have been isolated from any literature that is contrary to the thinking of Mao Tse-tung. What has been described as a 'cordon sanitaire' has prevented a whole generation of young Chinese from being contaminated with the terms of any other teaching. One who has been brought up in the Christian faith outside China, even though Chinese, would suffer more culture shock than a

Western missionary pioneering a work in an unknown tribe. He would not have to learn a new language, though the simplified Chinese characters might be strange to him. But there would be a new vocabulary and whole new thought system to be mastered.

Third, a returning Christian would need to accept a very strict discipline. The old way of life with its emphasis on individualism and freedom to make his own plans would have to be exchanged for a strictly regimented life motivated by one necessity, that of serving the people. Intellectual discipline would take the form of political and social re-education. His whole attitude to life would have to be changed. Through manual labour and long hours of indoctrination the old imperialistic thinking of the past would be rooted out. As a Christian he would have to learn thoroughly all the concepts of dialectical materialism, at the same time maintaining his spiritual life by faith in the Lord Jesus.

The indoctrination would be not only intellectual but emotional. Surrounded by masses of enthusiastic young people convinced that Chairman Mao has saved China from imperialism and the economic and social evils which formerly enslaved their country, the newcomer would have to enter into this atmosphere and display an ardent love for his country. He would certainly have to appreciate the appeal that Communism makes to vast masses of Chinese young people. Like most foreign visitors to the country, he would be impressed by the great material progress and the dedication of a vast population to a common goal under the present régime.

Many of the great economic problems of the past have been solved. The terrible inequalities between rich and poor have disappeared. No longer does a large segment of the population live under the threat of natural disasters such as flood or famine. The contrast between the 'bad old days' and the enlightened present would be stressed over and over again. Now there are none of the glaring inequalities which are to be found in a city

84

like Hong Kong with its great contrast between the very rich and the very poor. Many have been impressed by the clean streets, disciplined living and the absence of prostitution, sordid sexy advertisements and commercialism which are found in other parts of the world. Even though living standards may seem to be very low, the Communists have at least been able to provide for the basic needs of the largest national population on earth.

To paint Communism in completely black colours and to fail to appreciate its very real achievements will only close the door to any meaningful communication of the gospel. We must understand the pride Chinese people take in the material advances and in the restoration of China to an independent and powerful position in the family of nations. Chairman Mao in 1949 said it well: 'The Chinese people have stood up.' This self-reliance and the growing respect shown to China today by other nations is a swing of the pendulum from the humiliating experiences suffered during the days when Western powers had their 'concessions' and special privileges in China.

The Christian returning to live in China must match the enthusiasm he finds there in yet another sense. I well remember the singing, dancing crowds of university students in 1950. Their vast country was beginning a new era. There was no resisting the infectious fervour of their songs. It was the same feeling as that behind a more recent testimony of a member of a propaganda team in 1967, 'None of us were singers or dancers, but out of our deep loyalty to Chairman Mao and our infinite faith and veneration for him we went out into the streets, factories, communes and schools to spread the boundless, radiant thinking of Mao Tse-tung. We sang and danced with all our hearts.' Two years later in 1969 a commentator on Radio Peking described the enthusiasm of a group of workers with these words: 'They consider the spread of Mao Tse-tung thought as their most glorious task and most sacred duty.' James Reston of the *New York Times* after his recent six-week

85

visit to China was most impressed by the intensity of the 'evangelistic' moral fervour of the people. Speaking to fellow-journalists at the Foreign Correspondents' Club in Hong Kong he said, 'The nearest I can come to describing it is to compare it with my early Scottish Presbyterian Sunday School experiences.'

The first-century Christians considered the spread of the gospel of Jesus Christ as their most glorious task and most sacred duty. Without possessing the zeal and courage which characterized the lives of those who 'bore witness with great power to the resurrection of Jesus Christ', it is doubtful whether Christians can maintain their testimony in China. In 1950 it was only those students who possessed a joyful dedication to Jesus Christ and a vital fellowship among themselves who were able to make any impression upon their non-Christian friends.

Fourth, the Christian who plans to share the gospel with his fellow-countrymen must have a real spirit of love. He will have to face the Communist hatred of religion and will be deeply concerned for his brothers and sisters in Christ who suffer in labour camps. At the same time he must realize that Christians, both missionaries and Chinese believers, must accept responsibility for not fully revealing the Lord Jesus in all His purity and love. Too often the living witness of a sacrificial life has been missing. The disciple of Christ must therefore approach with all humility those who have been deceived by the prophets of materialism. They are men and women for whom Christ died, and the barriers of prejudice can only be broken down by love. They must be respected as fellow-human beings who are often very sincere in their efforts to find a solution to the problem of providing a reasonable standard of living for the 800 million who have lived under the threat of famine, war and flood.

The Christian witness living in a Buddhist or Islamic society would never start by attacking the religion of those to whom

86

he was sent, but he would faithfully, without compromise, proclaim the whole counsel of God. In the same way, the servant of Jesus Christ must courageously reveal Christ to his Communist friends, not denouncing their beliefs but positively showing that Christ alone can meet the needs of the whole man.

At the same time he cannot expect the Communist to react in the same way to him. 'You will be hated by all for my name's sake', said the Lord Jesus (Mt. 10:22). This statement is likely to be fulfilled in China, for the Communist system is diametrically opposed to the Christian faith. Christ and Mao can never share the same throne. For the Communist there is no room for loyalty to any other master outside of Communism.

Christianity and other religions may be temporarily tolerated for the sake of expediency, but ultimately the state will make war on all religions. Unless the Christian recognizes this, he may be led into a false optimism and be persuaded to compromise his faith for the sake of gaining some small favour from the state.

The Christian, therefore, must beware of an easy optimism. He must be prepared to have his message rejected and may well have to face persecution. Like Ezekiel, he may hear the Word of the Lord saying, 'I send you to . . . a nation of rebels, who have rebelled against me. . . . And whether they hear or refuse to hear (for they are a rebellious house) they will know that there has been a prophet among them. And you, son of man, be not afraid of them, nor be afraid of their words, though briers and thorns are with you and you sit upon scorpions' (Ezk. 2:3-6). The description, 'a nation of rebels', would certainly apply not just to Communist countries but also to other countries which have political systems that tend to turn men away from God. It is true, however, that under Communism rebellion is expressed more openly and causes severe suffering for the people of God.

Ezekiel was greatly disturbed by the message which was to

be delivered to this rebellious nation. Before starting to speak, he sat with them for seven days. He had seen the glory of God and knew that, while he must faithfully proclaim the message of truth, he first must be identified with the people to whom he was sent. The Christian in a Communist society may have to sit for hours listening to those to whom he is sent, in order to understand how to break down prejudice and reveal the message of the living God.

Christian witness and Communist ideology

The appreciation of certain thought patterns and emphases in Communist thinking will help the Christian witness in his approach. First, there is the very pragmatic attitude of the Communist leaders. They have little use for any teaching which does not lead to practical service to the masses. A speaker on the Shanghai Radio in 1970 quoted an earlier saying of Chairman Mao, 'How should we judge whether a youth is revolutionary? There can be only one criterion, namely whether he is willing to integrate himself with the broad masses of the workers and does so in practice.'

A Christian message which stresses only individual salvation and shows little interest in the needs of the masses will have little attraction for Communist youth. The Christian witness will have to be actively involved in ministering to the needs of the society in which he lives. Any suggestion of selfish individualism issuing from an over-emphasis on personal salvation and lack of concern for the masses will hinder people from considering the claims of Christ.

Many Communists would find it hard to understand the apparent selfishness of Christians. They would point to the fact that the Communist state does not allow a man to choose the place of work where he can obtain the maximum benefit for himself. He is sent to the place where his gifts can be used to serve the masses. Among the 'five goods' proclaimed over the Nanchang Radio in the summer of 1969 was 'good in creatively studying Mao thought and fighting self-interest'. What would Communists think of masses of Christian doctors congregating in the wealthy suburbs of the cities and neglecting rural or industrial areas? Or of Christian teachers who are not willing to teach in schools in remote areas or in the so-called 'lower class' sections of the city? I asked a Christian about the possibility of setting up a clinic in a large housing estate in an Asian city. He told me that his colleagues would consider it utterly foolish from the point of view of financial gain. There are indeed Christian doctors, teachers and engineers with high qualifications who willingly give up higher salaries in order to go to places where they can serve those who are in great need. It is likely that those who will gain a hearing among Communists will be those who have already demonstrated their love through self-sacrificial service without compulsion from governmental authorities.

It is, however, tragic that only a few Christian professionals demonstrate true dedication to the needs of society and victory over self-interest. Many would bitterly complain if deprived of their freedom and compelled by the state to serve where the need is greatest rather than where the salary is most attractive. This is not to suggest that we should set up a Christian system of regimentation that removes personal freedom, but God may sometimes call a Christian to choose the hard place.

Recently a non-Christian high government official in an Asian city poured ridicule on Christians who go overseas for training and then fail to return to help their own country. It is possible for safety, good salaries and modern conveniences to lure men away from their original goal. But the strength of Christian witness lies in the voluntary giving up of material gain in order to follow the One who came 'not to be ministered unto but to minister'. There is no merit in such ministry if it is only undertaken because the state imposes compulsory service.

A brilliant young Christian scientist, converted while study-

89

ing in America, returned to China because of his intense realization of his responsibility to his wife and family and nation. He wrote to me shortly before reaching Shanghai, 'I do not care whether I live six days or six years. I can only say with the apostle Paul, "I do not count my life of any value, nor as precious to myself if only I may accomplish my course and the ministry which I have received from the Lord Jesus to testify to the gospel of the grace of God".' If all Christians were motivated in this way we would not be put to shame by the accusation that 'Christianity is very good but it will not do for Asia for it is not sufficiently sacrificial'.

But, while showing that the Christian is not motivated by self-interest and is prepared to serve the people, one must also emphasize God's love for individuals. The gospel brings hope to individuals and then to society as a whole. The Communist emphasis upon the masses of the people often deprives the individual of a sense of real purpose for his own life. He may see himself as making a contribution to the future history of his people, but he himself is left without any hope after this life. The Communist might agree that a grain of wheat must fall into the ground and die, but, without any message of resurrection, each individual is left alone in the grave. His value as a man is limited to the few short years on this earth. For the Christian the new man and the new society are both present and future. Man's work begins in time and continues through eternity.

Chinese Communism's second characteristic, as we have already seen, is intense loyalty to the leader and dedication to the cause. After the initial success of the revolution in 1949, it soon became obvious that the teaching of dialectical materialism alone could not inspire people to sacrificial living. Their faith in the Communist movement had to be focused in a person. Acceptance of the principles of Communism had to result in complete consecration of the whole life to the cause of the revolution and obedience to its leaders. Disloyalty was the greatest of all crimes. A young Communist who later became a Christian described the tremendous demands that Communism made on him. He was indeed 'not his own' and was called upon to glorify the revolution and the party with all his being.

Unbounded enthusiasm for Mao thought causes the young Communist not only to sacrifice for the sake of the revolution in his own country but also to have a 'missionary vision': 'Oppressed people of the world will arise . . . the light of the thoughts of Mao shine on the whole world.'

A Christian with a lukewarm attitude to Jesus Christ has no message for an ardent young Communist. Only disciples of Christ utterly devoted to their Master, experiencing the reality of His presence and confident of His victory, can speak to the followers of Mao whether they be in China or in any other countries. Mao Tse-tung's life is drawing to a close. After his death Christians must be prepared to share their experience of the living Christ whose presence brings new life and new hope. His Lordship in every area of life and His love and uncompromising hatred of evil must be manifest in their lives.

Lastly, Communism is characterized by its world-view. The young Communist thinks in terms of historical developments and looks forward to the transformation of history through the revolutionary process. While Mao can offer no hope of immortality to the individual, he does call upon his followers to see the significance of their lives in terms of their contribution to history.

In a famous essay written in 1944 entitled 'Serve the People', Mao wrote, 'Serve the Chinese people. . . . Whenever there is struggle there is sacrifice, and death is a common occurrence. But we have the interests of the people and the suffering of the great majority at heart, and when we die for the people it is a worthy death.' Thus Mao taught that all men must die but that death can vary in its significance. A man's life and death can be a contribution to the dialectical process throughout the world. Such teaching is ultimately circular and does not explain individual significance. If an individual gets his significance from service to the masses, where do the masses get their significance? Surely only from the significance of the individual, but Communism recognizes only a collective significance.

In the Christian revelation, an individual is significant and valuable because he is made in the image of God. This is emphasized even more in the fact that Christ's death was described as being both for the individual ('the Son of God . . . loved me and gave himself for me'—Gal. 2:20) and for the whole of mankind ('the Father has sent his Son as the Saviour of the world'—1 Jn. 4:14). The Christian with a biblical world-view understands his significance in the light of God's over-all purpose in history. His hope for the future is summed up in Paul's words, 'The creation waits with eager longing for the revealing of the sons of God, . . . because the creation itself will be set free from its bondage to decay and obtain the glorious liberty of the children of God' (Rom. 8:19-21). Only then will the promise found in Revelation 11:15 be fulfilled: 'The kingdom of the world has become the kingdom of our Lord and of his Christ.'

With this confidence the Christian may indeed be enthusiastic about being caught up in God's great purpose which is being worked out in the history of our day. He knows that God is concerned for the nations of the world, and he recognizes that he is called to be a messenger of God's righteous judgment as well as of His mercy and redeeming love.

But if he lives in a Communist society, he will be surrounded by those who are convinced that Communism is the coming world system. To those who proclaim 'the kingdom of man', the Christian disciple must bring the message of another kingdom with the promise of the coming King whose reign shall know no end. This kingdom has already come, though it is hidden by the ugly shape of contemporary history. It is the eternal characteristic of the gospel that must challenge today's Communists. They would do well to heed the words of the playwright Eugène Ionesco: 'As long as we are not assured of immortality we shall never be fulfilled. We shall go on hating each other in spite of our need for mutual love.'

The Christian church today
The church in China today must show the real meaning of immortality and the practical nature of love. Her ability to survive will depend upon the vitality of the faith of Christians who remain. It is certainly impossible to estimate the size of the 'hidden church'. Exaggerated reports not supported by reliable investigation can only be harmful. There is no doubt that groups of Christians are meeting secretly for prayer and worship. Although only a few Christians have come out from China in the past few years, they are sufficient to bear witness not only to the continuing existence of a church but also to the fact that some young people have come to know Christ within Communist society and have been prepared to take the risk of meeting for fellowship with other Christians.

While it is true that during the Cultural Revolution the total suppression of all visible religious practices was regarded as necessary by the Red Guards, there is no indication that the official claim to hold to freedom of religion has been changed. To my knowledge, the most recent official statement was made by Premier Chou En-lai before the Cultural Revolution in a report to the Third National People's Congress, 21 December 1964.

'We shall continue to pursue the policy of freedom of religious belief correctly and to uphold the integrity of state power and the separation of religion from the state. We must prohibit all illegal activities. We hope that people in religious circles will continue to take a patriotic stand against imperialism, persist in the principle of the independence and self-administration of their churches, abide by government laws and decrees, intensify their own remoulding and actively take part in the socialist construction of our motherland.'

93

It is likely therefore that in the large cities certain churches may be allowed to remain open. Since November 1971 visitors have been able to attend mass in a Catholic church in Peking. More recently an English doctor has written a report and enclosed an order of service in the new Chinese script from a Protestant church which he attended in Peking on Palm Sunday, 1972. Numbers of Chinese attending these services are very small, and the congregations are mainly old people. Since most of the leaders of the Three-Self Reform Movement were not arrested during the Cultural Revolution it would seem quite possible that the government may permit that movement to continue in a limited way. This would not, however, make things any easier for the groups of secret believers who meet in homes, as any Christian activity outside the strictly controlled official church is forbidden. Those who visit China on official tours are likely to see only the official church, and contacts with secret believers could be harmful to them.

We may well ask what can be done by Christians outside China. Some time ago a pastor's widow, who has been imprisoned several times because of her continued activity in visiting and strengthening the faith of Christian families, wrote urging that Christians should continue to pray for the church in China. In spite of lack of information the members of the body of Christ throughout the world are called to share the burden of those who suffer in China. Somehow believers in China must be assured that they are not forgotten. Groups should be formed to study the situations in Chinese society and to pray for the spread of the message of Christ through the life and witness of His disciples.

No country is completely isolated. The Christian message can still penetrate Chinese homes through the radio. Those who prepare programmes bear a heavy responsibility and surely Chinese Christians who can read and write the language spoken by over one quarter of the human race need to do research and write scripts which will bear the mark of careful preparation and loving concern. Men must speak the message with the wisdom and power of the Holy Spirit.

There is a famine of the Word of God in China. The few Bibles which have survived the Cultural Revolution are in great demand. We have heard of the separate books of the Bible being torn out and passed around so that they can be copied. The present Chinese Bible is greatly in need of revision, and several groups including a Bible Society are working on a new translation. The New Testament has already been published in an edition using the simplified modern script. It is reported that copies are being sent into China while supplies are prepared for the day when doors are opened for the circulation of the Scriptures there.

At the same time there is an urgent need for Christian Chinese who understand the culture in China today to write books that will present the message of the living Christ. Books translated from the West or written by Western missionaries are not likely to be acceptable. Preparation of Christian literature should begin now so that it will be available when the opportunity arises.

During the next few years China's influence will increase in Asian countries. Her social and educational experiments will be discussed in every country. Even now many different delegations from south-east Asia are touring China and in the future we may expect to see business men, technical experts and educators from mainland China in the cities of Asia and Africa. Asian Christians there will need to know how to talk to them about the message of the gospel. Barriers of prejudice will have to be broken down, and this will be possible only as they meet committed Christians.

The youth of some countries are already strongly influenced by reports coming from China. Other areas in Asia may yet either come under Communist control or be ruled by a similar type of government hostile to the Christian faith. The church therefore needs to study the lessons learned by Christians in

China. Christians must know how to give an answer for the hope that is in them, and the church in every country should be prepared to continue her witness, if need be in different forms, regardless of political changes that may take place. The call of Christ to make disciples of all nations comes to the church in every generation. Changing political conditions can never excuse the church from fulfilling her commission.

A third of Asia's population lives under a Communist régime. They have been taught that Communism alone has an answer to the problems of life. Most of them have never yet been confronted with the claims of Jesus Christ. They can hear the message only when they meet those in whom there dwells the same Spirit who brought again our Lord Jesus from the dead. The Spirit alone can empower them to live and serve and if need be die in a Communist society. The love and faith shining forth from their lives will be a beacon showing the way to the living God who is still calling men to repentance and faith in the Saviour.